Science of *Happiness*

- the Theory of Positive Change

Jayanta Ghosh

SCIENCE OF HAPPINESS - THE THEORY OF POSITIVE CHANGE

iUniverse books may be ordered through booksellers or by contacting:

iUniverse
1663 Liberty Drive
Bloomington, IN 47403
www.iuniverse.com
844-349-9409

ISBN: 978-1-6632-1983-1 (sc)
ISBN: 978-1-6632-2635-8 (e)

Library of Congress Control Number: 2021916196

Print information available on the last page.

iUniverse rev. date: 08/18/2021

In loving concern for the human race

Contents

Introduction

It probably happens to most of us at times of our lives, that a vague feeling of unhappiness, a feeling of emptiness appears out of nowhere - even when you are doing quite well in the practical world! But you can't find the reason for this unhappiness! This can be frustrating, but there may also exist a blessing in disguise! Because, it may mean that your mind is healthy, and that it is searching for the real purpose of life! And, you have a hunch that the knowledge of this truth is the key to a deeper and lasting happiness! Your mind keeps on trying, but can't find it, and you get anxious because time is passing.

I had similar feelings intermittently in my life, starting in my senior high school years in India. It even made me leave my home intermittently, chasing 'holy men', and looking for answers. But I wasn't lucky enough to find them, and had to put my lingering thoughts in the back burner, and set my focus on my higher education.

After graduation, while I was pursuing my post-graduate studies in Electronics in the USA, those same old feelings of unhappiness started to haunt me again. They became more frequent and intense while I was pursuing my doctoral degree in Computer Science at

George Washington University in Washington, DC. They started to distract me so much that I decided to take a break from my studies, and dropped out of my course. I began doing some freelance photography, while exploring the source of my nagging thoughts.

Once, on a trip to India, I was standing on a riverbank. It was a real wide and slow-moving river with many inlets. I was standing near one of those inlets, reflecting on a few familiar thoughts. The water next to me was full of debris, made of lots of small logs, probably created by storms. I saw that most of them were bouncing into each other, becoming range bound and forming a stagnant pool. But some of them avoided hitting into each other, oriented themselves properly to catch the main flow in the cleaner water, and started to move forward with the river.

At that moment, a thought came to my mind that perhaps life has a natural flow like that of the river; and the purpose of life is to align or sync with it! And, there is a reward, which is lasting *happiness*! That is, if we are able to understand the main flow of life and align ourselves with it, we may be able to reach a state of mind, in which we can find many elements of happiness that we miss otherwise. Also, there may exist a much bigger purpose for this in our universe, which is even more important than our happiness!

But then, what is this *natural flow* of life? What is its objective? Where do we find the answers? Perhaps, the answers may be lying in some basic clues of life, which have been there all along in front of our eyes, but we just keep missing them! We think there is a lot more happiness waiting for us to be claimed in our lives - we just have to read those clues, and act accordingly!

Perhaps, there is a much deeper purpose for the existence of this pleasant feeling called *happiness* - its pursuit may be sustaining some vital projects in our planet. Perhaps, the way we pursue it has some very important and far reaching consequences. Perhaps, there may lie the secret mantra of our survival, as a specimen of life, extending indefinitely in our universe - into the very far future!

Chapter One

The Eternal Questions

One of the most profound questions of life is probably:

what is the purpose of life!

We feel a constant urge inside us to find the answer. If we knew the answer, perhaps we could plan our lives more efficiently with the right activities avoiding waste of time and energy through a multitude of unwise objectives, futile strategies and unnecessary conflicts. Perhaps, the answer could provide us the clues to solving most of our problems and make everything of life fall in place like the pieces of a puzzle. We all would probably start our life with enthusiasm, enjoy it with happiness, and pass away gracefully, handing the torch of life to the next generation seamlessly, each time enriching it with the wisdom of the current generation, without suffering any loss in the transfer!

Also, perhaps our destructive acts will be also be reduced, as most often they are generated while we are chasing the wrong objectives of life. Consequently, our mother ship planet earth would be preserved for the birth, growth and evolution of life for the maximum possible time. This would allow us more time to advance our knowledge and capabilities, perhaps enabling us to solve some of the most challenging mysteries of our real neighborhood, the universe. Also, the speed of our evolution will increase making us advance our capabilities faster.

But unfortunately, most of us have no clue about the true purpose of life, and probably only a few have any vague ideas about it. So, most of us look for some guidance from somewhere, and the most popular sources are the educational, spiritual and religious organizations. They provide valuable advices and instructions that basically recommend us to live a *good* moral life. They also talk about the benefits for following their instructions, which translate to *happiness* in one way or the other. Their guidance can be very useful in many situations of life. But, they have one uniqueness, which may be considered as a weakness by many. It is that generally they are based on faith, and not on logic or science. Perhaps because of this reason they fail to generate a serious conviction in many - specially in the minds of people who believe in science and logic. So, with the unanswered question in our heart we move forward in our lives without any solid conviction and try to enrich our mind with whatever spiritual help available.

The situation reminds me of an evening when I was traveling with my four year old granddaughter long time ago. I was driving home, and she was in the back seat of the car. It was getting dark; she was looking out through the car window. All of a sudden, she exclaimed, 'Dada, please drive faster, the moon is trying to fly away; please stay with the moon'. I said, 'okay, I will try', and started driving a bit faster. We were able to 'stay' with the moon that evening, and my granddaughter was very happy.

We probably try to 'chase the moon' all our lives to follow some mysterious purpose of life! We get involved in myriads of activities of different types and strategies to achieve this, but in spite of finding fragments of it here and there, a hunch inside keeps telling us that we have not solved the core of the mystery yet! But our mind says that it can be solved. Perhaps, we have to focus our acts in some special ways that are unique but not complicated! Thus, we collect the pieces of *wisdom* here and there, wherever available, thinking that they will provide the missing clues.

Though all the activities and efforts are great mental exercises for reinforcing our database of knowledge, perhaps the single most important act for 'staying with the moon' can be accomplished by opening the right 'window' of our mind. Perhaps, all we need to do is to know the simple but vital truth of life that we may have been overlooking all the time! Once we know this truth and assimilate it in our minds, we may be able to create our own *mantras* to suit our own styles of life in finding our fulfillment in our own unique situations. And, if this wisdom satisfies science and logic, it may draw the conviction, and perhaps create a common ground for science, philosophy and spirituality in a very significant way.

And perhaps, it will go even much further and make us see that there exists a much deeper purpose for the existence of this pleasant feeling called *happiness,* which may be holding the clue to not only our survival and prosperity on this planet, but to our long term survival in the universe in the very far future as a living entity!

The *urge* inside drives people to get involved in activities. They find happiness from certain types of acts. This reward of happiness make people keep on repeating those acts. Thus, the activities of life are created which constitute the *worldly affairs.* Perhaps, this reward of happiness has a direct relationship with how successful we are in following and satisfying the *purpose* of life! At different times of our

3

lives we probably achieve different amounts of success in following this *purpose,* e.g.:

a) We are totally in sync with the *purpose of life* using the right activities most of the time. The result is, our life rewarded with deep *happiness.*

b) We follow the *purpose of life* with our acts frequently, but deviate time to time; The result is, we get rewarded with reinforcements of *happiness,* but less than in case (a) above.

c) We keep moving away from the *purpose of life* most of the time.

The result is, we invite a life of misery.

Thus, it seems that there is a *purpose* of life which is latent, but is felt by all just like the influence of the magnetic force field on the magnetic compass to align with the force field. And, our happiness may be measure of our alignment with this absolute *purpose of life.* The directionality of our individual paths may be defined by our activities.

The pleasant feeling called Happiness

About 2700 years ago, around 600 BC, the Vedas and the Upanishads[27,28] started preaching an wisdom that said, attaining the state of enlightenment is the ultimate goal of human life, where unlimited happiness is found. A few hundred years later, at around 350 BC, the famous Greek philosopher Aristotle echoed the same opinion by saying that *happiness* is the ultimate purpose of human existence.

4

But, in spite of its most cherished status and the advancement of our science, the human culture has not been able to define the mechanism of happiness using any law of science so far! We are only familiar with its pleasant sensation, and have an instinctive feeling about the type of the activities that lead to happiness. Thus, since *happiness* is the driver of all activities, most of our activities of life are created not by wise planning, but by efforts of simple guesswork or instinctive assumptions! Some of these efforts become successful in finding happiness, and some don't. The successful ones create *positive changes* in our status and deliver happiness to us, while the unsuccessful ones possibly create *negative changes* and increase our chances of misery. Sometimes, the unsuccessful ones create excessive amounts of *negative changes* in the world around, and become known as destructive acts. Their negative effects accumulate over time. Thus, most of our destructive acts seem to be the results of our misguided efforts or shortcuts to find happiness of some form.

Generally, our activities in the pursuit of happiness consist of a mix of *positive* and *negative* acts. The *positive acts* help us find happiness and prosperity, while the *negative* acts increase the possibilities of problems and miseries for us. Generally, a person's concept of the science of happiness is reflected in the way the person pursues happiness through his/her activities. Thus, if someone believes money can buy all the happiness needed, the person's activities will naturally focus on making money. On the other hand, if a person believes that gathering knowledge will create *happiness*, his/her activities will be built around studies, research and other related activities.

Generally, happiness links with positive status changes. Different activities have different possibilities of creating *positive* and *negative changes* generating different intensities of happiness and misery. Thus, people chasing happiness in their unique ways are creating different amounts of *positive* and *negative changes* in the world around. As mentioned before, the activities that generate excessive amounts of *negative changes* become destructive acts. We live in a world where despite tremendous achievements created by the *positive* activities, destructive acts are accumulating at a furious pace which are creating threats to our survival on many fronts. Some examples of the major ones are overpopulation, extreme pollution, global warming, etc.. The problem of global warming appears to be creating the most serious threat to our planet through climate change. We can trace the origins of most of these problems to our mistakes committed in the pursuit of happiness! So, it is quite possible that most of these destructiveness could have been eliminated or reduced drastically if people could pursue happiness more wisely!

Thus it seems that all things of life are somehow linked to the uniqueness of our concept about the *true purpose of life* in some way because happiness is the reward for following this purpose correctly. Most often our concept of this purpose decides the type of activities we choose for the pursuit of happiness. Thus, having the right concept with conviction may be essential not only for the intelligent planning of our own lives, but also for all lives on this planet, as the well beings of all life are interconnected. Having the right concept about the *purpose* of life may also help us reach a state of mind that is more efficient in finding happiness. And, perhaps chasing this true *purpose* of life will lead us to the clues to our survival in this universe as a living entity!

Chapter Two

The Endless Pursuits

The pursuit of happiness seems to have started right at the beginning of life. At the lower levels of life this happiness seems to be physical in nature. Situated at the highest level of evolution, the humans pursue happiness in both, physical and mental ways. Some of the most ancient texts of wisdom like the Advaita Vedanta, which originated from the Upanishads, recommend people to go for the more advanced but difficult to achieve mental form of happiness. They have suggested some appropriate courses of training and activities to pursue it.

If we look around in our world, we see that beyond the basic necessities of survival, people get involved in activities to find some form of happiness. A person gets a job; it enables the person to make money, with which the person buys the elements of basic needs first; and then generally the person buys elements of *pleasure*, a form of happiness.

We go to a restaurant to find the pleasure of eating the food we enjoy. We listen to music we like, because listening to music gives us pleasure.

Parents love their children, because the act makes them happy.
We love the romantic activities, because we find pleasures and happiness of many types from those activities.

Thus, there are numerous examples of activities showing that they all originate while we are in the pursuit of happiness of some type.

Perhaps, the definition of the state of happiness can be broadened by including any kind of improvement of living status. Thus, even when we scratch our back to get a relief, it is an act of finding happiness. The *relief* being a form of pleasure, which, in turn, is a form of happiness. In fact, most of our activities are started to get some form of happiness - even when a criminal kills a person for no justifiable reason, he might be doing it to find a perverted form of happiness to satisfy his distorted mind!

In some situations, instead of looking for some direct elements of happiness, people go for the gain of power over others! Power gives a person the ability to influence others to act the way he wants them to. As a result, the person having the power can influence others to act according to his/her wish to create pleasure or happiness. Thus, power is a leverage to acquire the elements of pleasure/happiness more easily, and thus, the hunger for power is really the appetite for happiness, uniquely suited for the person.

And then, there are those of the other types, who go for the challenges of finding success in the projects they are pursuing. But, most of the times, they have the hope in the back of their mind that if they succeed, happiness will come through the satisfaction and also through the fame and fortune that may follow. Some of these folks are blessed with the extra talent and drive, and usually have a genuine love for the subject they are pursuing. They derive more happiness as they delve deeper into the subject. Quite often, these are the people who are pushing the boundaries of knowledge in different areas of life with passion, and quite often they succeed in almost any field they pursue.

Sometimes, while in the pursuit of happiness, folks get into conflicts with others. Often this happens when they are in disagreement about the sharing of some of the common elements of happiness. The real intention probably was just to claim their 'fair' share of happiness - the conflict starts when they aren't successful in getting it, or don't have the skill to make it happen! And, once a conflict starts, it seems to go on forever as the negative elements snowball. But, the craving for a harmonious and happy relationship with others always stays in the back of the mind. We also often employ negative emotions like hostility, jealousy, etc. to get our way, but probably the ulterior motive is always to acquire more elements of happiness as peacefully as possible. And then, we hoard money, hoping to be able to buy elements of happiness with it at our convenient time and place.

A friend of mine asked me, so what is the happiness to the person who commits suicide? The answer is that the person who commits suicide, most probably is in such a deep unhappy state of mind that the person doesn't see anything else but misery in his/her life going forward. So, to the person, ending the life may appear like a positive change or a 'relief', which is a form of happiness.

In today's world, sitting in our living rooms watching TV, we also see another unique type of activities. It is touching the lives of many in many different ways. 'Suicide bombers' are spreading terror all over the world! They are blowing themselves up with explosives, destroying places and killing many around. We may wonder how they find happiness in the act! They belong to a class of people who are committing suicide, while killing innocent people because of their political and/or religious differences! But the strange fact is that these people are also in the pursuit of happiness! Their beliefs, developed through misunderstandings and/or distorted preaching is making them extremely intolerant of others having different religious and/or political beliefs.

Another Identity of Happiness

It has been said by wise men that some form of *happiness* seems to be the driver of all activities of life! This becomes confirmed when we analyze the activities of the lower, simpler animals. We can see that happiness(pleasure) is the driver of most activities for them, and chances are high that this is true for all forms of life on this planet. The difference between us, the humans, and the lower level animals may be that, for them, the happiness comes mostly through physical pleasures, while for us it can come through both, the physical and the mental sources. The fox, for example, has three main basic activities - eating, mating, and protecting its territory. It derives direct pleasures from the first two activities, and these rewards of pleasure inspire the fox to repeat those acts. The third act makes the other two acts possible. The evolving ape was possibly exerting some extra effort in trying to reach some difficult to reach fruits, because he was finding pleasure out of eating them. And so he kept on repeating the act in the pursuit of this pleasure. Perhaps, this effort of the species was getting bolstered by improved capabilities created by beneficial biological changes due to random mutations happening over long periods of time. Thus, *happiness*, in some form, seems to be the driver of the most important project of life taking place on this planet, the *process of evolution.*

Since happiness seems to be the ultimate reward of life for following its purpose, a successful life may be rated in terms of the happiness found and created by its activities. These rewards of happiness come in many different forms and shades. Our life consists of a cluster of activities in the pursuit of happiness; once our time in life is up, we leave and another fresh life takes our place, and repeats the same routine. Thus, the amount of happiness we manage to collect in life seems to be a measure of how successful we have been in playing our roles. With this theory, it may be possible that an average person in an average family in our society earning an average income can be more successful than a very wealthy person in a very wealthy family! And, most probably, we all are very familiar with both types of people. Thus, our social hierarchy based on wealth may be truly artificial!

In this context, I fondly remember my high school Math teacher, who made Mathematics interesting to me for the very first time! And, he certainly achieved the same with many other students, to whom the Math class was a pure torment before. Initially, I also used to hate the subject; but later on, because of him, Math became one of my most favorite subjects. We used to get bored at the other classes, but wait eagerly for his Math class everyday. He used to start the class by giving us a short quiz to test our concept of the subject, and give out small prizes to the winners to raise our interest. These prizes were little things, like a fruit, a pen, or a story book, which he used to buy using his own money. This raised our competitive spirits, while at the same time improving our knowledge of Mathematics! But he was a very simple and friendly man, belonging to the low to middle income group, living in a very simple home. It became a popular spot for us - not just for his study helps, but also for his playful nature. His compassion and warmth were continuously expressed through his many activities with the student community. Though he didn't have much money, but was happy and full of spirit. So, he probably was a very successful person, helping many, and finding a high amount of happiness in his life.

Chapter Three

Different Roads People take

On July 22, 1995, in North Carolina, USA, a woman was convicted for killing her two young children by drowning them. She drove her car into a lake with her children trapped inside. She was trying to be united with her lover who didn't want the children!

In another real life story, on March 9, 2014, in New York, USA, a woman died of cancer in an unusual situation. The uniqueness of the story is that the woman came up with this terrible diagnosis when she was pregnant. Her doctor prescribed chemotherapy for her, but also told her that it might harm her unborn fetus. The woman didn't accept the risk on her unborn baby, and refused the treatment. Gradually, the disease progressed, and soon she was at a point of no return. After her child was born, she started her regular cancer treatments, but it was too late! In this case, the person placed her child's health before her own well being.

The normal lives of both women were disrupted - one through incarceration, and the other through death. But they had one thing in common - both were trying to find happiness. They used their own unique ways to reach their goal. But their plans were drastically different, showing very different mind sets and philosophies. Past human experience tells us that they had clearly different possibilities of finding a lasting version of happiness if they were able to continue their normal lives.

There may exist a yet unwritten scientific rule or law on the subject of happiness in any given situation which was violated by the woman in the first example, and was obeyed by the woman in the second example above. The chances of finding happiness seem to increase dramatically when we follow this rule, and decrease when we violate it. Perhaps, that's why, in the pursuit of happiness, some of our efforts are successful, and some aren't.

The above two examples probably represent two extreme cases. People pursue happiness in many different ways - sometimes they find success and sometimes they don't. One of my close friend's uncle recently passed away. He was known as a very hard-working and intelligent person. He was also a very wealthy person. Every time we visited him, he would give us advices on how to make money through smart investments, etc.. He helped many of his friends make money, and earned a reputation as a good financial advisor among our friends and neighbors. But, ironically, he never seemed happy himself - there was an air of unhappiness around him all the time!

On the other hand, there was my childhood teacher, a simple man, who chose to spend most of his time and energy guiding and helping his young pupils do well in and outside his classroom! He didn't have much wealth, and, most probably, had a pretty modest income. But despite that, he used to buy gifts and prizes for his students as encouragements using his own money. His system of awards and other encouragements helped us build our competitiveness and the foundation of future success. We also felt that he was very happy being our teacher. We always felt the warmth that he had in his heart for us, and always enjoyed his company tremendously. He has a permanent place in the hearts of mine and many of my childhood friends. Most probably, this type of people are very efficient in finding happiness or fulfillment in life in their unique ways. I think, most of us meet or know someone like him.

And then, there are millions of other people who choose to find happiness from the love and warmth of their family and their loved ones. Many of them probably work hard all day and return home in the evening to find the needed warmth and love, and then get ready for the next day's hard work. Thus, it seems, the pursuit of happiness is the primary function of our life; and people use many different activities and strategies, some of which are more successful than others.

Clues from Different Sources

We study numerous different subjects in our schools, such as, History, Geography, Math, Science, English, etc., starting very early in our life, and we have deep resources of knowledge on those subjects. But we don't find a course titled *Happiness101* in our school curriculums! And yet, perhaps it could have been one of the most important subjects in there. We want to find more *happiness*, and yet we are not getting taught on the subject in our schools, even when it is the most important thing in our lives! The situation is like investing most of our money in a financial product, about which we don't know anything! If we did, then we probably could learn its unique characteristics and its importance at an early age, and use this knowledge to find happiness more efficiently later in life. Perhaps, then we would behave a lot different in our pursuit of happiness, minimizing meaningless struggles and conflicts and other destructive activities!

Religion has given us many valuable advices for living the right way to be happy, but in many situations of life they may not be providing logical answers to why and how following those advices would make us happy! They may say that following their advices would please *God*, and in turn, *God* would reward us with happiness in many different ways, but this explanation may not satisfy the logical mind. The lack of logic in the answers creates a disconnect between religion and science resulting in a possible loss in conviction in the instructions of religion. And, this probably happens more commonly among the higher educated people who like to plan their lives following logic and science also. This is an important group of people who make the majority of contributions towards the advancements of science and technology through their innovation and creativity.

Another reason of people's lack of enough confidence in religion may be that the wisdom in religions is scattered over vast areas of texts, so that it may be difficult for people to find the appropriate answers quickly in their particular situations. People may want to check if their daily activities and decision makings are staying in the right path to lead them to happiness, and thus, they may be looking for a quick and simple answer to save them from the uncertainties. So, ordinary people may not be able to use them as often as they may want to.

Moreover, time to time in the history of the human civilization, the advices from religions have been vulnerable to distorted interpretations by people having hidden motives, other than truly helping the people. Many terrible wars have been started, and horrible atrocities have been committed in the name of religion, and this trend has not changed yet.

Also, everything changes with time. After passing through the boundaries of time, space and cultures, the interpretation of the original message of wisdom can change in some very important ways - more so with the globalization of modern times, when people of different countries and cultures are coming and living closer together. Consequently, some of the original religious instructions may gradually develop different interpretations and thus cause confusion instead of harmony. Therefore, to be effective, they may need to be checked, clarified and updated periodically. But, it seems that those actions would be extremely unpopular and almost impossible to implement.

Thus, with the available wisdom and lack of conviction, folks try to build a code of conduct themselves, and hope it will be useful in their pursuits of happiness. But they suffer another setback when they start seeing plenty of examples of others violating the code of conduct, and yet living seemingly happy and prosperous lives! Our confidence takes another severe blow, and they may feel the urge to ignore the traditional wisdom themselves! For example, here are some of the well known advices from some of our popular religions:

Honor your father and your mother.

You shall not commit adultery.

You shall not covet. (to desire (what belongs to another) inordinately[12])

Avoid those actions which harm the mind and impede spiritual development. Hurt none by word or deed.
It is not only necessary to understand the teachings; it is also necessary to apply it to our own needs.
Admit your ignorance
Practice what you preach

Don't become attached to this world(material).

We know that all the above guidelines are extremely beneficial, but they are violated quite frequently by people in today's world. And, it is most likely that in spite of those violations, people expect to be successful and find happiness in their lives through their unique routine of activities! This probably shows a lack of conviction in our moral guidance.

The failure to find a dependable clue to finding happiness in life often makes people wander around aimlessly, making them feel frustrated at times. Perhaps, this is the reason why, sometimes, a vague feeling of unhappiness persists in our mind, even when we are prospering in the material world! There may exist a sneaky suspicion in the back of our mind that is telling us that our ways of chasing happiness may not be the right ones! So, we start experimenting with a multitude of different types of activities - getting some satisfaction and happiness here and there, but perhaps not with the certainty that those are the right ways! Then, while trying different activities we may get involved in some truly unwise ones that invite serious misery! And, chances are high that this probably is the pattern of activities many of us follow!

In Maryland, USA, we had a neighbor, I will call him Benny. He was a computer engineer, and had a very good job at a prominent corporation. He had a dazzling home, a gorgeous wife, couple of new cars, and two beautiful children, a boy, and a girl, who were attending the local high school. Benny seemed to be doing real well with a beautiful family around him. Then, in his pursuit of happiness, he began experimenting with some different activities - he started gambling. He started visiting the Atlantic City Casinos in the weekends. The guidance from available wisdom clearly condemns gambling activities. But, in our society this advice is ignored quite often, and gambling is a fairly popular pastime! Gradually, Benny became addicted to gambling and his activity increased - both he and his wife started going to the Casinos. The children were left behind under the weak supervision of their old grandparents, who were fragile and very mild-mannered, living in an isolated corner of the mansion.

The kids started going bad, mixing with the wrong crowd and getting involved in destructive activities. They began to fail in their classes, and their lives soon took a downhill spiral. Their son started to have problems with the law, and was temporarily suspended from the school. The daughter began dating multiple boys, and eventually became pregnant. But, Benny still couldn't break his addiction to gambling, and kept on going to the Casinos together with his wife, leaving his children alone! Gradually, the demise of the children started to ruin the happiness of the entire family, and the family begun to have problems in other areas of life. And, there are plenty of similar examples!

Thus, there is a true need for a effective set of guidance while we get engaged in the activities of life in our pursuit of happiness. This guidance needs to be simple but sound, and also needs to have the support of science and logic; because they help to reinforce its foundation, and help people develop conviction in this code of conduct.

Chapter Four

Is there a Supreme Force!

Many of us, with or without using some form of logic, believe in the presence of a *supreme force* casting great influence on our lives on this planet. They call this *force* by many different names like *God, Jehovah, Bhagavan, Allah,* and so on. These folks tend to believe that this *force* wants us to behave in certain ways, and if we follow these directives, we will be rewarded with happiness in many different ways. They try to develop a concept, generally with the help of their religion, and try to follow its guidance. Often they tend to develop a *faith* which overrides their logic and intelligence in many of the important decisions of life. But then, there is also the other group of folks who do not believe in the presence of any such *supreme force* controlling their lives. They try to live their lives by depending on logic and science. Thus, a fervent topic of debate has been created in our societies, which has many important implications. But it is not too difficult to decide which side wins the argument logically!

The Force Field of Life

We all know from science that our planet is a part of the huge universe around us. We live in an environment which contains enormous sources of cosmic energy and force. The Sun is the dominant one in our planetary system; it is radiating a tremendous beam of energy on our planet. Life is starting, it is flourishing and getting engaged in the activities of life; the process of evolution is taking place. Through this vital process, life forms are advancing their capabilities, exploring newer territories for habitation and improving their survival to face the challenges of the constantly changing environment. In the process life is evolving higher. Also, some are becoming extinct when they are failing to develop the required skills to survive in their environments. Thus, holistically, a gigantic project of activities is taking place on our planet. Science says, there is always a force behind every activity. Therefore, it is a scientific fact that a *supreme force* is behind all the activities of life on this planet. Like other forces, this immense force has created an gigantic force field that is shrouding our planet. Let's call this the *force field of life,* as it is the source of all life on this planet.

Pattern caused by a Force Field

Another sign of the presence of a force is displayed by the presence of a pattern in the behavior of its subjects. A *force field* can be defined as the influence or the effect of a force on its subjects in its active area or the *domain.* Inside its domain the force field wants its subjects to behave in certain ways and it opposes other types of behavior, creating a pattern in their behavior. We see the presence of a few different types of forces on our planet whose force fields are causing patterns in the behavior of their subjects. One of them is the magnetic force field. When we pick up a magnetic compass and set it on the top of a table, it feels the effect of the earth's magnetic force field urging itself to align with the magnetic force field by orienting in the north-south direction, and the compass complies. Then if we forcibly displace the magnetic compass from this position, it enters a turbulent state of oscillations or vibrations until it gets back to its *in sync* state of the north-south orientation. Thus the magnetic compass displays its interaction with earth's magnetic force field and its two states of existence - the *in sync* and the *out of sync*. When the compass is in sync with the magnetic force field, its status is stable and peaceful. We can call this the *happy* state. When it is out of sync with the force field, its status is turbulent or *unhappy*. Thus the magnetic force field causes a pattern in the behavior of the magnetic compass.

We see the presence of another force field on our planet caused by the gravitational force. When we drop a piece of a rock, it doesn't act randomly by moving upwards or sideways, but falls towards the ground. It is behaving that way because of the presence of the gravitational force field. This force is guiding the motion of the rock to fall straight towards the ground. This pattern of motion defines the direction of the gravitational force field. When we disrupt this pattern by trying to stop or move it in any other direction, *turbulence* is generated in the form of pressure or impact from the rock, and also possibly through noise and other associated effects. Thus, the stable *peaceful* state of the rock is its motion straight towards the ground. Then it is aligned or in sync with the force of gravity.

In both cases above, the subjects display a pattern in their activities because of the influence of the driver force field*s*, which urge them to get aligned with them. When they are taken out of this alignment, instability and *turbulence* ensues until they get back into the stable state, in which they are in alignment or in sync with the driver force field. When the subjects behave in the approved ways, their efforts make them in sync or in line with the agenda of the force field; and when they act in unapproved ways, they are *out of* sync or in conflict with it. When in sync, the subjects find a peaceful or *happy* existence. When out of sync, the subjects face a conflicted, turbulent or *unhappy* existence.

The Force Field of a different kind

Like other force fields, the *force field of life* is also exerting its influence on its subjects. It is urging all living things to get in sync with it. That is, it is influencing all life forms on this planet to promote its agenda of birth, growth and evolution. Higher evolution of life seems to be its main objective. It is influencing the physical states of life forms to promote evolution as is described by the science of evolution pioneered by Charles Darwin[13]. Evidence shows that the *force field of life* is also influencing the states of our minds by influencing its happiness and unhappiness in predictable and logical ways - we increase our chances of happiness when we stay in sync with it, and we decrease our chances of happiness or increase our chances of misery when we get out of sync with it. Therefore, it may be important to know how to get and stay in sync with the *force field of life!*

The magnetic and the gravitational force fields mentioned above induce clearly defined patterns in the behavior of their subjects. The *force field of life is* also causing a pattern in the behavior of all life forms on this planet - their activities revolve around an urge to live, grow and evolve through acts of eating, mating, protecting their territories and other similar acts. Their routines of activities help them survive and prosper while at the same time delivering pleasures(happiness) to them. If they leave this routine, first of all, they won't get the pleasures of life, and then they may not be even able to survive on this planet. The life forms come back to find more pleasures, and repeat the routine of activities. Thus a pattern is created in their behavior, in which one type of activities lead to survival and prosperity, while other types may lead to danger, struggles and probably to death. And, the important point is that the life forms are guided instinctively towards the right type of activities by the lure of happiness(pleasure) in some form. Thus, they find pleasure from the act of eating while the act supports their survival.

They find pleasure from the act of mating while the act supports the survival of their species. Thus a pattern is generated where the right act that supports their well being and the survival of their species while delivering happiness to them. This pattern, in turn, promotes evolution.

Thus, the *force field of life* mostly created by the Sun is inducing a behavior pattern in the activities of all life forms. They are instinctively guided towards the right activities. The *instinct* seems to be a product of the influence of the *force field of life*. All life forms are born with the *instinct*, but probably its presence is most clearly manifested in the behavior of the lower animals, who have not yet developed an advanced intelligence to interfere with their natural guidance system provided by the *instinct*. Often, animal babies start exhibiting this instinctive behavior right after they are born, well before learning anything from their parents. Also, animal parents, specially the mothers, show the effect of this *instinct* by trying to save their babies at all cost - even at the expense of their own lives! The immediate objective of this tremendous urge seems to support the survival of the species so that it can live and take part in the project of evolution, the ultimate purpose of the *force field of life*.

The behavior of life forms under the influence of the cosmic *force field of life* appears similar to the behavior of the magnetic compass under the influence of earth's magnetic force field in the sense that they both try to align with their driver force field. The magnetic compass orients itself in the north-south direction which is the direction of the magnetic force field; and the life forms choose a path of life, growth and evolution, which is the directionality of the force field of life. Thus, a natural code of conduct exists for all life forms on this planet, and they try to follow it as faithfully as they can. The rewards are the pleasures(happiness) of life while their activities help them evolve and survive the challenges of their environment.

The influence of the cosmic *force field of life* on life forms is manifested in numerous ways, but probably the most important evidence are the physical changes happening to them through the process of evolution as explained by Charles Darwin's famous theory of evolution[13]. Evidence shows that this force field is also exerting its influence on the state of our minds - our happiness and the miseries are affected by it in ways that can be defined using logic and science, and this knowledge can make a significant impact on the ways we live and find our *happiness*. This may have the potential of creating some positive changes to human cultures that can have some far reaching implications affecting our activities and our survival in the very far future!

Chapter Five

The Science of Happiness

It appears that we don't encounter feelings of happiness or misery just randomly - a certain type of outcomes of activities or events leads us to happiness, and, on the other hand, a different type creates misery for us. And, if we analyze the nature of these activities, we may find that, in general, the two groups of activities have clearly different characteristics. Activities or events that lead to happiness tend to create *positive changes* in our status; while on the other hand, activities leading to misery create *negative changes*. And, generally we instinctively know what is *positive* and what is *negative* for us. Thus, since we are naturally attracted towards happiness, we select the type that generates happiness, and stay away from the ones that lead to misery. Thus, a pattern is created in our behavior as mentioned before, which shows that like the magnetic compass in the magnetic force field, we are also getting guided to stay within a pattern of activities.

Thus, we have used laws of science and logic to show the fact that we are living inside a tremendously powerful cosmic force field, the *force field of life*, which has been created mostly by the enormous cosmic energy of the Sun. All life forms on this planet are products of this energy. Thus, each of us individually is made of a fragment of this cosmic energy enclosed inside our unique material body. This energy inside us is creating different types of *personal individual forces* which are displayed through our various activities, both physical and mental. These *individual forces* are *vector quantities* having magnitudes and directions, which are changing constantly depending on the nature of our mental and physical activities.

Looking at the history of life forms, we can see that the mental part of this *individual force* is progressively becoming more dominant as we evolve higher with advancing intelligence. At any certain time, the *direction* of our *personal individual force* is defined relative to that of the *force field of life,* and is defined by the nature of our mental and physical activities at that time. Thus, this *individual personal force* can be in sync or out of sync by various amounts at any certain time. For example, when our activities promote the survival or prosperity of life, the direction of our *personal individual force* is mostly in sync with the *force field of life.* Basically, *positive acts* that promote the prosperity and well being of life help us stay in sync with the force field. Some good examples of *positive acts* are activities that deal with love and nurture, because they promote survival and prosperity of life directly. Other *positive acts* help the well being of the human race, and perhaps all life on this planet in some way. On the other hand, acts of unnecessary violence resulting in harm and destruction of life and prosperity make us out of sync with the *force field of life.* Of course, there are activities that are in between, i.e., they are moderately *positive*; e.g., helping someone in need and so on. Thus, all our different activities that represent our *personal individual forces* have different degrees of sync or alignment with the cosmic *force field of life.* Also, the *personal individual force* for us, the humans, changes its direction quite frequently. Because being guided by our highly active mind, the nature of our activities changes often. Consequently, we are constantly interacting with the cosmic *force field of life* with different degrees of alignment.

The Science of Interacting Forces

Science has discovered what happens when two forces in the same domain with varying amounts of sync interact with each other. When they are in sync or in line with each other, they are mutually supportive of each other, and their interaction is peaceful. On the other hand, when they are out of sync or not in line with each other, a conflict takes place often resulting in a turbulence, whose intensity is proportional to the amount or the degree of the misalignment. Thus, two forces having varying degrees of alignment will have conflicts of various intensities.

For example, when someone is swimming in a river, it is much easier to swim in the same direction as the river's flow, than against it. Then the person can move faster or go further with the same amount of effort than when swimming in the opposite direction. Here, there are two forces in action - one is that of the river's flow, and the other one is the swimmer's effort to go against the flow. When the person is swimming in the same direction as the river's flow, the force of the flow promotes the swimmer's effort. Then the swimmer can swim further and/or faster with the same effort than when swimming in the opposite direction. When swimming in the opposite direction, the force of the flow works against the swimmer's efforts creating a conflict. This causes a turbulence, making the swimmer apply more effort to go the same distance, and also get tired sooner than when swimming in the same direction as the river's flow.

Similarly, our *personal individual force* is constantly interacting with the *force field of life* with continuously varying degrees of sync, depending on the nature of our physical and/or mental activities. They will be either in sync, in partial sync, out of sync, or partially out of sync with the *force field of life* at any certain time, depending on the nature of our activities. Therefore, according to the rules of science of interacting forces, the resulting outcome will vary from being peaceful or *happy* to turbulent or *miserable* with varying intensities. Also, the nature and the intensity of this outcome would depend on the nature or the degree of the alignment of our *personal individual forces* with the *force field of life,* and we would have the possibilities of feeling the effect through various sensations, from the pleasant feelings of *happiness* to the unpleasant feelings of *misery*. These feelings may take place in many different forms and intensities, and also they can be instantaneous or delayed. We, the humans, have an extensive and complex response system for these feelings which may act as buffers, slowing down or completely inhibiting these feelings temporarily, but the potential may continue to grow.

Thus, the cosmic *force field of life* shrouding our planet has a profound effect on our minds. All our happiness and miseries at any certain time are linked to the nature of our interaction with the master *force field of life* at that time in clearly defined ways; and it is possible to increase or decrease our chances of happiness(and miseries) by controlling the nature of this interaction. This can be achieved by controlling the nature of our mental and/or physical energies by controlling the nature of our activities, and thereby controlling our degree of sync with the master cosmic *force field of life*.

Chapter Six

Staying in Sync - the *Theory* of Positive Change

Thus, it is important that we make a serious effort to get in sync with the *force field of life.* Science says that for an activity to get in sync with the controlling force field inside its domain, the activity has to be in the same direction as the master force field. The direction of an activity can be defined in different ways. One way is by its motion or orientation towards something or some point. Thus, the magnetic compass stays in sync with the magnetic force field in the north-south orientation. But the *direction* of a force field can also be determined holistically by the nature of its activities. The direction of the *force field of life* can be defined this way. This force field is promoting positivity of life through the birth, growth and evolution of life on this planet. Its ultimate objective clearly seems to be the higher evolution of life. Evolution is built by an unending chain of minute *positive changes* to life forms over long periods of time. According to the science of evolution, pioneered by Charles Darwin[13] in the mid nineteenth century, life forms are evolving through a series of beneficial or positive physical changes happening to them. These *changes* raise their survival capabilities, and thus, they can be called the *positive changes*. Thus, the element of *positive change* is the building block of the process of evolution as it demonstrates the core virtue of the project of evolution carried out by the master *force field of life* shrouding our planet. Therefore, to stay in sync with this force field, we need to express similar virtues through our activities, i.e., the activities need to promote or create *positive changes* - however simple those acts are, and however minute those *changes* may be. In fact, it is possible that the *positive change* may be so miniscule or subtle that we may not even be able to notice it! We may only instinctively know that we are applying our efforts in the *right direction* through our mental and/or physical activities.

Thus, it seems that the concept of the *positive change* and the capability to sense it are vitally important for staying in sync with the *force field of life,* and in turn, for finding happiness. These capabilities are almost instinctive with life forms - specially with the simpler creatures. We, the humans, often modify these instinctive capabilities with our advanced intelligence, sometimes adversely affecting them. Perhaps, that's why the human ways of finding happiness is infinitely more complex than the lower animals. Perhaps, our advanced intelligence gives us a capability to promote higher evolution more vigorously, and thus find infinitely more happiness, but we are also much more prone to mistakes and the resulting misery! We are also more on our own, since at our level we probably can't depend on our instinct! Following the *positive change* may be the most reliable way of planning our activities in the pursuit of happiness.

A *positive change* can be created or promoted by acts which can vary from the most simple type like eating food to the most complex type like self-sacrifices for a higher cause, etc.. This subject of *positive change* has been explored in more details in the next chapter. One of the most important requirements of the *positive change* is that it has to be a positive status change not only for the individual self, but also for the overall species, mostly in the most minute ways, so that it promotes its survival, and in turn, its evolution. Obviously, a *positive change* cannot be harmful to the species. This requirement applies to all life forms.

Sensing and following a *positive change* appears to be a natural skill of a life form. It is carried out almost totally instinctively by most life forms except man, who often lets his advanced intelligence overtake his instinct. The lower animals seem to create *positive changes* effortlessly through almost all of their activities which consist of eating, mating and protecting their territories. The activities are beneficial for the self as well as for the overall species for promoting their survival. Thus, these activities of the lower animals faithfully keep them in sync with the *force field of life*, and consequently, deliver happiness to them, mostly in the form of physical pleasures.

For the humans, on the other hand, not all activities in the pursuit of happiness create or promote *positive changes,* because some of them may not be overall beneficial for the human species. For example, many big wars between nations have been big producers of *negative changes*; similarly, many scientific/industrial projects have also produced *negative changes* by adversely affecting our environment! Thus, we get involved in many activities that do not help us improve our degree of sync with the *force field of life*. Consequently, many of our activities in the pursuit of happiness do not deliver us true happiness.

There may be many different reasons for we, the humans, to behave like this; but one of the main ones may be that often we have the tendency to settle for a lower quality happiness called *pleasure* in stead of going for the true happiness, if it needs less effort. Most of the items of pleasure belong to the hedonistic[48,49] type of happiness, and may not always create *positive changes* in the world around. Even when they do, they generate low amounts of *positive changes* - some of them even can generate *negative changes,* and invite misery in the long run! The activities in the pursuit of only the eudaimonic[48,49] type of happiness seem to have the possibilities of creating *true positive changes*. There are also acts of hedonistic happiness which do not generate *negative changes* and can be safely included in our list of activities in the pursuit of happiness. We have explored these in more details under the topic, *Different types of happiness - the Secondary Sources*, in the chapter, *Discussions*.

The ability to sense a *positive change* appears to be instinctive. The instinct seems to be a product of the effect of the *force field of life* on life forms. It helps creatures to know what is *positive*, what is *negative*, and what is a *positive change* for them. Parental guidance and life experiences probably reinforce this natural sense. For the lower animals, instinct seems to help them in most of their activities. They follow this sense extremely faithfully, as is clearly demonstrated in their behaviors. The role of intelligence started to become progressively more dominant in higher animals, which seems to help them survive and prosper in more complex situations of life more effectively.

It appears that compared to the lower animals, we have minimized the use of instinct as our automatic guidance system. Instead, we use our intelligence to make the decision. It seems that we use our instinct to sense the *positive* and the *negative* paths in a situation, and then use our advanced intelligence to try to follow the path selected. But our situations can be immensely more complex than those of lower animals, and our advanced intelligence can often contradict our instinct. In this type of situations, we generally override our instinct with our intelligence and behave in complex ways. Also, compared to the lower animals, our list of activities has expanded tremendously; so the determination of a true *positive change* for a human can include many variables; but for most cases sensing the *positive* path still seems to be straight forward and instinctive. We have tried to explore this subject in more details in the chapter, The Positive Change.

Summarizing the theory of happiness and the theory of positive change:

A) *All life on this planet are living inside an immense cosmic force field of life created mostly by Sun, which is causing their birth, growth and evolution. We are constantly interacting with this force field with our energies represented by our various physical and/or mental activities and receiving results.*

B) *Acts in sync with the force field of life promote the force field, and cause peaceful interactions, generating the possibilities of the pleasant feelings of happiness. On the other hand, out of sync activities create confrontational interactions, generating the possibilities of turbulence in the form of the unpleasant feelings of unhappiness.*

C) *We can stay in sync with the force field of life and thus increase our chances of happiness by creating or promoting positive changes in various areas of life in mostly extremely minute ways through our daily regular activities.*

As mentioned earlier, the most unique and important requirement of a true *positive change* is that it has to be beneficial(*positive*) for the self and also for the greater world around(species), even if it may not be *positive* for some, or even many! This way it promotes the survival of the species, which is its ultimate objective. This has been discussed in more details in the next chapter, The Positive Change.

The science of interaction says that the intensity of the feelings of happiness at any certain time is expected to depend upon the degree of sync of our *personal individual force* at that time with the *force field of life*. As mentioned before, our degree of sync is determined by the nature of our physical and/or mental activities, which can be improved by selecting the activities that promote the agenda of the *force field of life, i.e.* activities that create *positive changes* by supporting the well being and survival of the human species.

The theory describes the basic mechanism of happiness, the actual process may be significantly more complicated because of the multitude of the various combinations of different activities in which we get involved to create the *positive changes*. Each activity may contribute its own share to the over all status change. Also, the multitude of the elements from which we derive our pleasure or happiness add to the complication. Most of our activities generally create a mix of *positive* and *negative* changes - mostly in very minute ways. The net or the overall *change* due to the activity in a certain period of time would be the determining factor for the happiness or the misery caused by that activity in that period of time. There are numerous real life experiences, which can be used as examples supporting this theory. Some of them have been discussed later, in the chapter of the Case Studies.

Chapter Seven

Some Implications of the theory of happiness

a) Happiness and its link to material wealth:

Perhaps, one of the most important implications of our theory is that it can help to liberate the mind from the popular concept that happiness is proportional to the material wealth possessed. It achieves this by showing that the foundation of happiness is really built upon the creation of *positive changes,* and not on the possession of excess wealth beyond a certain basic amount. And, these *positive changes* can be generated in many areas of life where the help of material wealth may not be needed. For example, *love* in its many different forms is the primary driver of *positive changes.* A basic amount of wealth, of course, is necessary, because it guarantees the physical survival of a person by providing the safety and the well being of the person, and thus they create the most important initial *positive changes.* But beyond that, the mind's ability to find happiness does not seem to depend on the possession of extra wealth. To the contrary, it can adversely affect the happiness of the person through introduction of negative elements like the egos and the anxieties and the resulting stress which are commonly associated with the fear of losing the wealth. Happiness seem to rely more on the attitude and the efforts through various different activities that not only benefit the individual, but also promote the well being of the greater world around, i.e., on the creation of *positive changes*. A very interesting study on the subject of *happiness* has been presented in details in the documentary, *Happy*, directed by Roco Belic, released in 2011.

This correction to the popular concept can be very useful as it can liberate the mind to grow in whatever direction it chooses, and the person doesn't have to be wealthy to be really successful! People can follow their passions and aptitudes to choose their professions, and contribute more efficiently to the human evolution with innovations of all types that create *positive changes*. Thus, once the logic and science of the mechanism of happiness is understood and assimilated, people may start feeling this unique sense of freedom. They may start feeling that the promises of their lives are not limited by their monetary status any more, and that reaching any heights are possible, and it is truly up to them!

This liberating effect of the theory can be extremely powerful. We are just beginning to realize that *happiness* is the magical nutrition for our well being - not just for the mind but also for our body. Our theory of happiness and *positive change* says that it may be possible to find almost unending supply happiness from almost unlimited sources that can create *positive changes*. This seems to have the potential to revolutionize the human culture because people may fight less for material possessions, and instead apply more efforts in developing the mind so that it can find alternate ways of finding happiness by creating *positive changes* in other numerous areas of life.

Our theory also confirms the conventional wisdom that *happiness* is better than *pleasure*, because activities associated with *happiness* create *positive changes* which benefits the species by promoting its survival and thus promoting evolution, while activities associated with *pleasure* do not necessarily create *positive changes*. People find pleasure from eating an ice cream and they also find happiness from helping a homeless kid; the difference between the two is quite obvious.

Our theory of *positive change* clearly explains the difference between the two types of happiness categorized by modern psychology, the eaudaimonic[48,49] and the hedonistic[48,49] types. The theory says, to build a stable foundation of happiness, pursuit of the eaudaimonic type of happiness is preferable to the hedonistic type, because, generally, the activities in search of eudaimonic happiness has the potential for creating more *positive changes* than the hedonistic type. In fact, if folks do not use extra caution in selecting the element of pleasure, the activities pursuing hedonistic type of happiness can create *negative changes!* A merchant can make money by selling products which may be overall harmful to the world, and then he can buy elements of pleasure with the money! We have explored this subject in more details in the chapter, Some Random Thoughts, under the topic, Different types of Happiness - the Secondary Sources.

Finding happiness from the eudaimonic sources seems to be a bit more difficult than finding it from the hedonistic sources - even if the quality of the latter may be inferior. The difficulty probably lies in the fact that compared to the hedonistic sources of happiness, the eudaimonic sources offer a kind of happiness that may require more effort. The happiness obtained may also seem to be a bit more subtle and mild in general. The flow of happiness may also start more slowly than the hedonistic type. But like the ocean, it may start shallow but gradually can lead to tremendous depth. The happiness from hedonistic elements may start out fast and intense but generally is shallow and fading quickly.

b) The theory creates a common ground for Science and Religion:

We all know that a feud is going on between Science and Religion for a long time on the subject of evolution. There has been a creation-vs-evolution debate in Kentucky on the 4th of February, 2014 where Bill Nye, the science guy met Ken Ham, the founder of the Creation Museum. But is Science's theory of evolution really going against Religion? Let's analyze the subject a bit to listen to the important points that both sides are saying, and see if they are contradicting each other!

The first thing Religion does, is try to make us believe in the existence of a supreme force *God,* who controls everything of life. Science, on the other hand, says that a supreme cosmic force created mostly by Sun is causing the birth, growth and evolution of life on this planet, which controls just about everything of life. So, the concept of Science about the presence of the supreme cosmic force is parallel to the concept of *God* in Religion.

Next, Religion has built a code of conduct for us, and told us that if we follow this code, we would please *God,* who in turn would reward us with happiness. This code of conduct includes advices for us to live our lives in certain ways to find happiness. If we analyze these advices properly, we can find that they are suggesting us to get involved in activities that are traditionally known as *good deeds.* If we analyze these *good deeds,* we can see that they basically are same as the *positive acts* that create *positive changes* in the world around us. On the other hand, our theory, based on logic and science, shows that activities creating *positive changes* find happiness. So, basically, they are saying the same thing.

We also have shown before that the nature of the force field shrouding our planet is *positive* for life, which implies that activities that bring *positive changes* increase the possibilities of finding happiness. On the other hand, activities that create negative changes increase the possibilities of inviting misery. Religion says the same thing!

So, it seems that Science and Religion, both believe in the existence of a supreme power in our lives; and they both conclude that when we promote the creation of *positive changes* in the world around us, we are rewarded with happiness. Thus, Science is not really opposing Religion with its theory of evolution. To the contrary, it may, in fact, be providing a scientific and logical foundation to the beliefs of Religion.

Our theory also provides a useful tool as a by-product of its analysis. It probably happens quite often that some folks following religion rigidly misinterpret its guidance, and pursue a line of activities that will benefit their smaller inner circle but harm the greater world around! By doing this, those folks will create *positive changes* for their group but *negative changes* for the greater world creating overall *negative changes*. In a similar way, people of science can also pursue scientific or industrial activities that can benefit their inner circle but create an overall harm for the world. According to our theory, the presence of a net *positive change* is an indication that we are on the right track, because then our activities are staying in sync with the *force field of life*. They are then promoting evolution and inviting happiness. The theory also adds a requirement to the definition of the so-called *good acts* that are supposed to bring happiness. A *good act* should generate overall *positive changes* in the greater world around. This requirement also creates some guidelines to our beliefs - our beliefs should be such that they would encourage us to get involved in activities which create *positive changes* in the greater world.

Thus, our theory of *positive changes* may have some truly important applications. Looking at the past history of the human race, we can see that instructions of religion have been misinterpreted repeatedly. They have been used as excuses for some of the worst atrocities in this world. People have been getting brainwashed constantly by clever preachers having hidden agenda which are far from the true purpose of religion. Similar things happened on the side of science also. Scientific knowledge have been misused routinely on projects which produced monetary profits for a few with very little gain to show for the true well being of the human race! They have created *negative changes* through pollution, global warming and many other serious problems which are threatening our future survival on this planet. Thus, our *theory of positive change* creates a overall check for all our activities, be it religious, scientific or any other type. It may be able to help us evolve higher faster, reducing our destructive acts to preserve our mother ship planet earth much longer. And for the immediate reward, it may help us find more happiness in our lives.

c) The theory provides a scientific and logical base under Positive Psychology:

Positive Psychology, the newest branch of psychology pioneered by Dr. Martin Seligman and others in late 1990's has made a significant contribution to the perpetual effort of mankind to establish a code of conduct for people in their pursuit of happiness and well being. It has evoked a great deal of interest, specially among the well-educated and well-to-do circles of folks. Seminars and courses are being offered in prestigious institutions to help gain mastery of the subject, and then use it in everyday life. We hope that this knowledge gets circulated to the general public also, who can benefit from it, and raise the usefulness of the knowledge.

But the subject is quite similar to religion. Religions have been preaching very similar advices to people starting from very early stages of human civilization. They were meant to guide people to the *right ways* of living to find happiness. These recommended ways of living were determined mainly from past human experiences under various situations of life. In other words, they were based on empirical evidence, not on any rule of science. And, the knowledge from these data was further enhanced by the wisdom and intuition of a few extra-ordinarily gifted people. Thus, the religions developed guidance which are supposed to be helping people to live right. But, some of their beliefs were built on assumption, not on logic or science. It is possible that this lack of support from logic or science could have compromised their ability to demand conviction from people. Thus, in general, even though huge number of folks follow religion in one way or the other, many do not develop real conviction in it. Consequently, people violate their guidelines quite easily and frequently for various reasons.

Positive Psychology, on the other hand, uses a rigorous and organized study of statistical data using advanced tools of precise record keeping. Also. they do not use the element of faith to support their findings. Thus, its advices and suggestions are much more realistic and less ambiguous than those of religion. But the overriding similarity between them is that like religion, Positive Psychology also uses empirical evidence. That is, its database is built on observation, experimentation and record keeping of human experiences under varying conditions of life, rather than from any theory or law of science. Thus, most of the time, it can predict what activities and behaviors will lead to happiness and what will lead to misery from its database; but it does not provide the scientific reasons why they will do so. In other words, it can't explain how the feelings of happiness and misery are generated using laws of science.

Empirical evidence generally provide discrete data as opposed to facts derived from laws of science. Scientific laws generally produce continuous data with almost unlimited data points. An empirical database, on the other hand, generally present information with possible missing data points. Thus, one possible drawback of the empirical database is that it needs to be extensive to include all possible situations of life. Positive Psychology offers an empirical database providing answers for discrete situations of life; thus gaps may exist in its database. Consequently, the results may not be given with confidence outside the known set of variables. To increase the accuracy of the database, the number of data points may need to be increased. It seems that Dr. Seligman has done exactly this procedure on the presentation of his theory! In his book Authentic Happiness, he has presented the initial data set by providing answers for a discrete set of variables; and then, when he found that it didn't cover some situations of life, he provided more data points in his later book, Flourish.

In the book, 'Authentic Happiness', Dr. Seligman expressed his theory on happiness by saying:

"happiness could be analyzed into three different elements that we choose for their own sakes: *positive emotion, engagement,* and *meaning*.".

Then he thought that the theory had some 'holes', and needed more data to patch them up. This he did in his later book, 'Flourish', in which he included the additional data points for *happiness*, which are *relationships* and *accomplishments*. Our theory of happiness and *positive changes* derived using laws of science and logic supports the concept of Positive Psychology, but our theory says that this action was not necessary. The element *meaning* or *purpose* of his original theory generally includes the elements of *relationships* and *accomplishments*, because a *positive purpose* usually also requires the elements of positive *relationships* and positive *accomplishments*.

Our *theory* says that the foundation of happiness is created by creating *positive changes* in the world around. To accomplish this we need the following elements:

a) Positive attitude: this is similar to 'positive emotion' as explained in 'Authentic Happiness'.

b) Activity: this is similar to 'engagement'.

Positive attitude and activities are used to create:

c) *positive changes*

And, when it says that we have to create a *positive change,* it implies that we have to control *positively* many factors that influence the generation of the *positive change.* Among them *meaning(purpose)* and *accomplishment* are built in the meaning of a *positive change,* because without them we can't determine what kind of change it is. The other factor, *relationship with others* is an important element for the creation of *positive changes.*

The activities of life are numerous and diverse, and they keep on changing constantly. Thus, an effective guidance has to deal continuously with changing situations of life. Theories that are derived from or supported by laws of science are generally more efficient in providing answers for continuously changing variables. Our *theory* has been derived from laws of science and logic; and thus it is applicable in most situations of life. The theory supports the findings of Positive Psychology; and in addition, it perhaps also provides a logical and scientific foundation underneath this field.

Mihaly Csikszentmihalyi, another pioneer of Positive Psychology, thinks that an unique state of mind leads to happiness. He named it *flow*[39]. He said:

"The best moments in our lives are not the passive, receptive, relaxing times . . . The best moments usually occur if a person's body or mind is stretched to its limits in a voluntary effort to accomplish something difficult and worthwhile".

Here, the word *worthwhile* should be underscored as it has some important implications. According to our *theory of positive changes,* it defines the direction or the nature of *flow.* Activities creating *flow* should also create *positive changes* in the world around because they link with happiness. Aimless activities that create *flow* in random directions may not necessarily lead to sound happiness, as the benefits of a few of the inner circle may come with the overall harm of the greater world around creating conflicts and wastes of energy. We find an example of this situation in Positive Psychology pioneer Martin Seligman's book, Flourish. Dr. Seligman was talking about some folks playing the card game, Bridge. These folks were playing the game with intensity, and often seemed to be in the *flow.* But from their behavior they didn't appear to be happy! They used to try to win at all costs, and their acts in the game often looked mean spirited and narrow-minded. Our theory says, even if they were in *flow,* it didn't have the right direction, because the acts were not creating *positive changes.* Thus, they were not really happy. If they were playing in a manner that created a friendly enjoyable environment for all or most of the players, it could have produced *positive changes.* Then the *flow* would have been *positive,* and probably would have invited happiness.

Science is advancing by leaps and bounds and is helping people develop progressively more capabilities to improve the survival and well being of the human species. But, the *negative changes* like the pollution, global warming, extreme inequality, etc. are also growing fast along with the *positive changes*. They are adversely affecting the overall status change for the human species, and causing serious threats to their future survival - and perhaps to the survival of all life on this planet. Unless this trend is stopped, we may face extinction on this planet well before our science can be advanced enough to find a way for our survival in this universe!

It seems that our destructive activities are actually the results of our misguided or unwise efforts to find happiness in some form! So, it seems vitally important that we chase happiness in the right ways. Here our theory of *positive change and happiness* may provide a scientific and logical guide for finding happiness in the *right ways* in almost all of our activities. This may help us stay in sync with the *force field of life*, increase the speed of our evolution, enhance our survival capabilities and find more happiness in our unique situations of life. This may also help us preserve our mother ship for the longest possible time, and perhaps raise the possibility of us becoming a living entity in the universe in the very far future!

Chapter Eight

The *Positive Change*

Our theory says:

The feelings of happiness and miseries are experiences that are generated as the results of the interactions between the cosmic force field of life shrouding our planet and our personal individual forces defined by our physical and mental activities.

When our personal individual force is in sync with the force field of life, the interaction is peaceful, generating the possibilities of the pleasant feelings of happiness in many different forms and intensities. On the other hand, when it is out of sync, the interaction the unpleasant feelings of unhappiness.

The enormous cosmic energy mostly due to the Sun has created an immensely powerful force field which is shrouding our planet, and is causing the birth, growth, prosperity and evolution of all life on this planet. We have called this force field, the *force field of life*. The evolution of life is being caused through a stream of minute *positive changes* to life forms. Thus, positivity is the nature or the property of the *force field of life*. So, we promote this force field, or get in sync with it by promoting positivity through our physical and mental activities. We also contain parts of that same energy inside us that is creating our own personal individual forces. At any certain time this personal individual force of a person has a direction, which is defined by the nature of his/her mental and physical energies expressed through mental and physical acts. Activities creating *positive changes* or pro-growth activities obviously make this direction more 'in sync' with that of the *force field of life*. On the other hand, destructive activities creating *negative changes* make this *direction* deviate and more out of sync with the *force field of life*. Thus, we can increase our possibilities of finding happiness by creating or promoting *positive changes* in the world around us through our regular everyday mental and physical activities.

The *positive changes* generated by the activities of life forms promote their evolutionary processes. For lower animals these status changes are mostly physical in nature; for us, the humans, they can be both, mental and/or physical. Generally these *changes* are extremely minute, and often the mere attitude of promoting these *positive changes* can create the proper chemistry of the mind, which is needed to create the right environment, conducive for generating more *positive changes* in the world around us. This *positive* attitude of the mind increases its alignment with the cosmic *force field of life*, and consequently it finds happiness from the simple things of life that are often overlooked by others.

In the stone age, the humans were creating comparatively fewer *positive changes*, and as a result, the speed of human evolution was comparatively slower. It gradually picked up speed as we evolved with time. Now, in this age of advanced technology and knowledge, our evolution has taken off exponentially. Theoretically, there is no reason why this process can't continue indefinitely into the very far future making us develop newer capabilities to meet the newer and more difficult challenges of the environment, survive and evolve higher. But, then, there is this requirement that we have to keep on creating a steady stream of *positive changes*. Perhaps, there exists an important, far reaching purpose for the evolution of life on this planet! Perhaps, it is to survive indefinitely into the very far future as a living entity of the universe!

The speed of our evolution is proportional to the rate of *positive changes* created by us. With a faster speed of evolution, we are able to develop newer or more advanced capabilities faster, and pass through higher stages of evolution quicker. This may be an important requirement for our survival in the universe in the far future, as the life-sustaining qualities of this planet may last only for a definite amount of time.

It appears that all creatures are born with the instinct that guides them to recognize what is *positive* and what is *negative* for their well being. Thus, when the options of possible *positive* and *negative* status changes are offered to life forms, they instinctively choose the path of the *positive* status change with the appropriate actions. This selection promotes their survival and well being. This instinctive behavior is more clearly seen among the lower animals as they lack the advanced intelligence to interfere with their instinct. Their instinct helps them create *positive changes*, while finding happiness(pleasure) at the same time.

Thus, the *instinct* works as the natural sense to differentiate the *positive* from the *negative*. It seems to be the natural urge of all life forms to align with the *positive* with appropriate actions. Our theory says, the *instinct* is the result of the influence of the cosmic *force field of life* on life forms. It is an urge created inside all life forms to get in sync with the master *force field of life* with appropriate activities in different situations of life. The effect is similar to that of the magnetic force field on the magnetic compass causing it to get in sync with it in the north-south orientation.

Lower animals follow their instinct quite faithfully with their simple activities of life. We, the humans, follow our instinct in much more complex ways. Generally, we get the cue from the instinct about the *positive* line of action, and then, unlike the lower animals, we use our advanced intelligence to follow our line of actions. This has proven to be much more effective than following the instinct alone, as has been shown by the history of our civilization, and also by the fact that we are at the top of the evolutionary ladder. But in spite of these accomplishments, our advanced intelligence shows frequent vulnerability to the influence of many factors driven by emotional, social, cultural, economic and many other elements. They often prevent us from making the correct decision that could optimize the production of *positive changes*.

An Analysis of the Positive Change

In the absolute sense, a *positive change* can be defined as a *beneficial* status change happening to a life form that helps its survival, and in the long run, the survival of the species. The well being of a life form generally depends on its survival; and so a *positive change* generally promotes the well being of a life form.

Status changes can happen in many different ways, and they can have the potential of becoming beneficial, but they generally need to be utilized with appropriate activities to become *beneficial* status changes or *positive changes*. One prime example is the status change caused by biological changes that have been happening to life forms through minute random mutations. When used with appropriate activities, these status changes become *beneficial* to the life form, and thus they become *positive changes*. They provide the life form competitive advantages over others through the *natural selection*[13],as explained by Charles Darwin's theory of evolution; thus boosting their survival capabilities. Thus, it can be said that the evolutionary level of a species of life form is basically proportional to the amount of *positive changes* happening to it. These *positive changes* help a creature develop newer or advanced capabilities; and since the survival, well being and happiness of a life form are all interconnected, we can say that a *positive change* for a living being tends to promote its prosperity and happiness. Also, an increase in the survival capabilities of a life form is generally caused by an increase in the range of activities of the creature; and thus, the evolving creature stays in sync with the cosmic *force field of life* with increased routine of activities with expanded elements of happiness.

Changes in the status *or* the status change*s* for life forms are happening continuously in our immediate world, and in the greater world around us. Some of them are produced by our activities. Accordingly, we can control the outcome in those situations. But some others are created by elements beyond our control, and we can only moderately influence its effect on us through our activities. Many of the status change*s* happen extremely minutely and we hardly notice them, but they influence our lives and our survival in complex and subtle ways. And then, there are the dramatic status changes caused mostly by the forces of Nature over which we don't have any control. But in most cases, the activities of the creature can influence the nature and the depth of the outcome to some extent most of the times.

As a simple example, our rivers are getting choked with pollution caused by the trash dumped into them, and thus a *negative* status change or simply, a *negative change* is being created by our activities. The situation is getting worse with time creating larger and deeper *negative changes*. And, it will keep on getting worse if nothing is done about it. But, the outcome can be controlled if peoples' behavior can be controlled by persuading them to reduce the amount of pollution they are causing, and thus the depth of the negativity of the status change caused by the pollution can be reduced. Thus, our activity can influence the severity of the *negative change*. Status changes caused by most external factors can also be influenced by our activities. For example, the devastation of a future earthquake can be reduced by enforcing proper building codes and other maintenance and restoration acts.

The potential of a status change to be beneficial is accomplished when the benefit is utilized by appropriate activities. Then the status change is converted to a *positive change* which promotes happiness and well being. In the big picture, a *positive change* promotes evolution by improving the survival of the species. To get a clearer picture of how a status change and the activities of the creature relate to the process of evolution, we need to take a look at the earlier stages of evolution, where a status change and its role in the generation of the *positive changes* are clearer.

Let's consider the case of evolution of the venomous snakes[25] from their previous non-venomous status. Here, a status change happened to the snake through biological changes, because of which the snake could produce venom inside its body, and inject it to its prey through its fangs. The benefit potential of this status change was utilized nicely by the snake's activity of finding food by subduing the prey by biting. In the previous non-venomous status, it seems quite probable that the snake used to lose some of its potential victims because they were able to escape even after getting bitten. Furthermore, probably, the snake itself also used to get injured by the struggling victim often in the process. But now, the venomous snake can just bite and release the victim and then wait for it to succumb to the effect of the poison. This way it can avoid any possible injury, and also kill its prey more effectively. Thus, a huge *positive change* was created by the biological change, which has given the poisonous snakes a tremendous competitive advantage for survival, and they have prospered on this planet.

Here we can see a possible flowchart of the process of evolution:

1) a status change was created by a potentially beneficial *biological change* happening to the creature, probably just by chance, and

2) the status change was utilized by appropriate activities to create a competitive advantage for survival; i.e., it was converted to a *positive change.*

Thus, we can see that the use of appropriate activities are essential for utilizing the potentially beneficial status changes to create *positive changes* needed to create competitive advantages, which in turn promote evolution. And, this is more critical for the us, the humans, in our advanced stages of evolution, as we will see later in this discussion.

A potentially *beneficial biological change* is one which generally opens up a new area of activities for the creature. Thus, we can say:

Positive Change => *Potentially Beneficial status change x Appropriate Activity*

Where '=>' means 'depends upon'.

And, since:

Evolution => *Positive Change*
Evolution => *Potentially Beneficial status change x Appropriate Activity*

Except in the cases of drastic external status changes created by forces of Nature, the survival of a species depends upon its evolution, which happens mainly through beneficial biological changes through random mutations[26] over time. The species generally gain newer capabilities through evolution to survive the challenges of its environment. Thus, we can say:

Survival => Evolution
=> Beneficial Biological Change x Appropriate Activity

Since the life form has no control over the beneficial biological change, we can say:

Survival => Appropriate Activity

Thus, we can say that the survival of a species depends upon the use of appropriate activities which can utilize the potentially beneficial biological changes, and convert them into *positive changes.*

The status changes can be happening to a species of life forms through external factors or internal random biological mutations. In both situations, proper activities are needed to convert these status changes into beneficial or positive changes. Status changes through external factors are rare occurrences, and are generally caused by forces of nature. The famous Chicxulub asteroid crash of 66 million years ago is a prime example, which was disastrous for most creatures living above ground, many of whom perished. The event created a tremendous *negative* status change for them; but it created opportunities for some smaller creatures living underground, whose competition diminished and the territory expanded immensely. Thus, the event created a huge *positive* status change for these creatures. They prospered, and over time created new branches of animals through evolution.

Science says, a very different type of status changes have been happening to life forms since the start of life through very slow and gradual biological changes. They seem to be happening continuously but randomly. These beneficial biological changes have provided the creatures competitive advantages in some areas that promoted their survival. For the lower animals the vital competitive advantages have been happening in the basic areas of activities of eating, mating and protecting their territories. Here, the creatures had to go only through a short list of activities to find the appropriate activities that would be able to utilize the potentially beneficial biological changes. So, the appropriate act is quickly selected, and the status changes created by the biological changes are converted into *positive changes* promoting their survival.

But, for the humans sitting at the top of the evolutionary ladder, the task of finding the routine of activities that would be able to utilize the potentially beneficial biological changes is extremely challenging. Because they are happening in the area of the intelligence, which are not physically obvious; and thus can't be detected easily. Even after they are detected, an extensive and rigorous routine of activities may need to be tried before the appropriate activity or the routine of activities are found that are able to utilize the beneficial biological changes. We have discussed this topic further later in this chapter.

An external status change can be beneficial or harmful to a creature. It is beneficial, when the activities of the creature can take advantage of the status change, and make it an aid to the survival and prosperity of the creature and its species. On the other hand, it can be harmful when the *change* is detrimental to the survival and well being of the creature. Similar to the biological status changes, an external status change can become a *positive change* with the use of proper activities.

The famous Chicxulub asteroid crash of 66 million years ago created a huge status change for most creatures. It caused the extinction of dinosaurs and most other large creatures, because their activities of life couldn't extract any benefits for survival or *positive changes* out of that immense incident. Thus, it was the ultimate *negative* status change for most creatures who lived aboveground and perished. But for some other smaller creatures who lived underground, the disaster created some opportunities or beneficial status changes. These smaller creatures were able to dig their way out of the disaster and carry on their activities of life, and thus their survival was not affected by the calamity happening above ground. Once their survival was assured, they found many significant *positive changes*. The threats to their survival diminished dramatically, and their territories increased enormously in size above ground, as their competition for food had perished in the catastrophic explosion. Thus, they took advantage of the immense status change using their unique abilities and activities of living underground, and converted it to a huge *positive change*. As a result, they prospered and enjoyed the pleasures of living, and started whole new evolutionary branches of life, that eventually produced today's human. Thus, the Chicxulub asteroid crash of 66 million years ago created different kinds of status changes for different species of creatures.

The *positive changes* happening through status changes seem to take place in inter-species as well as intra-species ways. In the inter-species ways, they favor one or a group of species of animals over others, giving them a survival advantage over other species. Probably, the majority of this type of status changes are caused by events or changes in Nature that cause habitat changes, affecting different species in different ways - helping some and hurting some. Normally, the favored species prosper and dominate in time over others in the race for survival. Then, probably, further evolutionary processes happen on those species lines using the intra-species type of status changes. The Chicxulub asteroid crash incident is probably the most extreme example which produced both, *positive* and *negative* inter-species status changes.

The intra-species type of *positive changes* normally happen when an individual or a group of individuals within the same species develop beneficial status changes, mainly through naturally happening biological changes, providing them a competitive advantage over others. Thus, the individual or the group of individuals dominate over others in the same species, and then pass on these beneficial biological features to their descendents through reproductive activities promoting evolution. Normally these intra-species beneficial changes seem to happen through minute biological mutations, which, science says, have been happening mostly randomly.

When the early woodpeckers originally used to look for food, they probably didn't use their activity of digging into the tree trunk as much. Also, probably their beaks were not as big or strong as the present day woodpeckers. Like most life forms, probably they were also having minute biological changes of various types happening randomly, but perhaps, most of those *changes* were coming and going without making a lasting effect on the species because the typical routine of activities of the bird did not utilize them. Then, when a physical change of a slightly longer and stronger beak happened, it was quickly utilized and transformed into a *positive change* by their activity of digging. It gave the bird a competitive edge over other birds because of finding of a new territory, the tree trunks, from where they could find food. The individual or individuals having this *physical change* dominated their species and prospered. The species focused their activities on this feature of a sturdy beak, which got stronger with each generation. Gradually this feature got transmitted to their descendants through reproduction. Thus, here the potentially beneficial status change created by a longer and stronger beak was utilized by the appropriate activity of digging into the tree bark to create the *positive change*, which helped the bird evolve.

According to science, biological changes have been happening to life forms from the beginning of life on this planet, and have been occurring through minute mutations, either happening randomly or caused by some environmental factors. They have been creating subtle status changes, some of which are getting utilized through appropriate activities turning into *positive changes,* increasing the survival capabilities of the creature. But, not all of the biological changes that are happening randomly are getting converted to *positive changes,* because they may not be getting utilized by the creature using appropriate activities. For example, it is possible that some finch chicks are being born occasionally with a slightly longer beak by chance, but this physical change may not be getting converted to a *positive change* because the feeding activities of finches normally do not use digging.

But, it may also be possible that a new physical feature generated by a physical change can spur the start of a new activity that may create a new survival aid or a *positive change* for the species, which can promote its survival. Thus, it is also possible that in the future, a new group of finches may appear with a longer beak and start a new activity of digging and eating worms in addition to, or in stead of eating seeds! This may start a whole new evolutionary branch originating from the finches, which may look and act different from the original finches.

Minute biological mutations have been happening in different parts of the body, as well as in the brain areas. Looking at the living world, we can deduce that for most of the intellectually advanced creatures, the important biological changes have been happening in the areas of the intelligence. The changes that have been happening in other parts of the body have been important for the lower animals because these *changes* improve their physical competitiveness, which plays a vital role in their survival efforts. It appears that as the creature evolves higher, it becomes progressively more challenging for the creature to detect and utilize the beneficial physical changes with the appropriate activities because they are difficult to detect. And, this may be most applicable to the humans.

Chapter Nine

The Routine Activities, Ability Circles and the Process of Evolution

Since the start of life, *positive changes* have been happening to life forms, gradually over very long periods of time, and have been the building blocks of the process of evolution. They have been raising the survival capabilities of life forms, and probably would keep on happening as long as life thrives on this planet.

To the living world, the main attraction of life is *happiness* in its many different forms, which includes pleasures of many types. These elements of happiness are acquired through many different types of activities that create *positive changes* promoting the survival and the evolution of life forms. The creature becomes familiar and fond with these activities as they become its routine activities. These routine activities generally define the capabilities of the creature as it tries to find as much happiness(pleasure) as possible safely from its activities.

This becomes clear when we look at the simpler animals situated at lower levels of the evolutionary ladder. Different kinds of activities are available to them in their everyday lives, some of which can create *positive changes* for them, and some others generate *negative changes,* i.e., some activities can benefit them, and some others can harm them; but they instinctively select the ones that are *good* for them, i.e., they create *positive changes* for them. In other words, they normally select the acts which offer them happiness(pleasure), and which are safely within their capabilities that assure their safety and well being. Thus, when presented with both possibilities, *positive* and *negative*, they select the *positive acts* producing *positive changes*.

For example, when a weaker animal is confronted by a much stronger animal, it has two options. It can stand its ground and get involved in a fight risking its life, or it can protect itself by fleeing. Except in unusual situations, the weaker animal flees to protect itself. This act of running away is beneficial for its survival, and thus it generates *positive changes* for the animal. There are numerous other examples where both, the *negative* and the *positive acts* have the equal possibility of being selected, but the creatures instinctively chose the *positive acts*.

Thus, most of the times, creatures instinctively select the activities that are proven and safe producers of *happiness.* Accordingly, these activities promote the survival of the species, and thus they produce *positive changes* for them. In an analogy, it's like while moving forward on a road and coming to an T-intersection, where one has to turn left or right to stay on the road! Undiscovered and undeveloped area lies straight ahead of the T-intersection. Most of the animals of the species repeat the same proven activities most of the times, and thus their activities stay within a circle, the radius of which is the distance to the T-intersection. Let's call this the *Ability Circle* of a creature. The animals normally stay within their *Ability Circles* using their routine activities. Then, once in a long while, a creature is born in the species with extra talents. Like other animals in the species, the creature reaches the T-intersection while repeating the routine activities of the species. Then he faces the unknown territory ahead which requires additional skills to survive. But with his extra talents, the creature goes through the intersection to the unknown area and survives. He discovers a new territory, perhaps finds new elements of happiness, and in the process, the creature extends the radius of the *ability circle* and evolves higher.

The radius of the *Ability Circle* of a creature is proportional to the sum of all his survival skills. Let's call this an *Ability Index*, which is an indicator of the survival capability of the animal, and is the sum of all his survival skill indexes. Let's say, just for an example, that the survival skill of an animal is roughly composed of the following hypothetical survival skill indexes, on a scale of 10:

	Bird	Fox	Human
The primary abilities:			
a) Ability to find food >	7	7	9
b) Ability to protect from other animals >	3	5	9
c) Survival ability in changing environment >	3	5	9
d) Ability to reproduce in challenging habitat >	3	4	9
...			
Totals (Ability Index) >	16	21	36

Thus, the bird scores 16, the fox 21, and the human scores 36 out of 40. So, the bird will have the smallest of the three *Ability Circles*, while the human the largest. Each species may occupy a narrow band of circles, depending on the variation in abilities between individuals in the species. The bird species may occupy a band of circles; the species that includes foxes similarly may occupy another band of circles of radius larger than that of the birds. The human species has the longest radius; so it occupies the topmost band of circles.

Generally, creatures live their lives by finding pleasures that are available through their routine activities, e.g., the acts of eating, mating and protecting their territories and other activities in various forms. Most of their activities in search of pleasure take place within the boundaries of their respective *Ability Circles,* which are defined by the limits of their capabilities. The radii of their respective *Ability Circles* increase as their capabilities increase.

Creatures are constantly trying to find more pleasure through activities by extending the limits of their capabilities by stretching their *Ability circles.* But they are not successful until they develop some extra capabilities, which would create *positive changes* in their status. With the newer capabilities, now the creature can try a new activity in the pursuit of pleasure outside the boundaries of safe routine activities and still survive. With this new activity the creature does not take the same type of turn at the T-intersection of his *Ability Circle.* Instead, he chooses to move straight ahead to go out of his *Ability circle*, and starts to track a new circle with higher radius. Thus, the radius of his *Ability circle* is increased by his increased capabilities. An increase in the radius of the *Ability Circle* may mean that the creature has evolved.

Generally, these *extra capabilities* are gained from some of the randomly happening biological changes, which are utilized by appropriate activities and converted to *positive changes.* This becomes clear when we use the previous example of the evolution of the poisonous snake. It evolved from the non-poisonous status, in which state it had to bite and then hold on to its prey to find its meal. Most probably it failed many times, and it lost its meal often; and also, most probably the snake got injured a few times through the struggle with the prey. The efficiency of the snake improved dramatically when it developed the capability of developing the deadly venom inside its glands and then injecting it into its prey. Science says that this capability was acquired through gradual biological mutations happening inside the snake, every step of which was probably promoted by the activity of the snake of finding its food by subduing its prey by biting. Now, after it became poisonous, the snake could just bite its prey once, and then release it, avoiding injury to itself. The prey succumbed soon by the action of the poison, and the snake could eat it at its leisure. Here, the activity of the snake ideally suited its biological changes, and converted them to *positive changes* promoting its evolution from the non-venomous to the venomous state. This extra capability helped to stretch the *Ability Circle* of the species.

But not all biological mutations promote the survival of the species, and in fact, some may generate *negative changes* in their status, adversely affecting their survival prospects. For example, the albino tiger lost some of its survival capabilities because of losing the natural color of camouflage in its natural habitat. The Kakapo parrot of New Zealand is another example. The bird evolved in oceanic island environment, where the predators were scarce, and the food supply was abundant. The ability to fly in its natural habitat was not required for survival. So, over many generations of gradual physical changes, it lost its ability to fly. But then things changed dramatically for the bird, when the rapid industrialization of the world increased overseas traveling. People brought cats, dogs and other predatory animals as pets to the island, who preyed on the birds. Without the ability to fly, the Kakapo parrots became easy targets. Their predicament worsened when people hunted them for food and decorations. Consequently, the bird population plummeted and almost reached the *extinct* status. Currently it is on the *critically endangered* list. Therefore, the biological changes in these cases generated *negative changes*, which reduced their survival capabilities, which, in turn, reduced the radii of their respective *Ability Circles*.

An increasing radius of the *Ability Circle* of creatures may imply that evolution is happening. Once a creature evolves, it traces a new *ability circle* of higher radius. This expands the creature's capabilities and his area of activities, which, in turn, increases the sources of happiness(pleasure) of the creature. The creature then pass on the newer capabilities to the next generations through reproductive activities, and an evolution of the species may take place. At present, the creature having the largest *Ability Circle* is, of course, man with his advanced brain, which developed over many generations of gradual *positive changes*. We know that these kinds of *changes* are the building blocks of the process of evolution of life, and they are continually stretching the A*bility Circles.*

Human Ways of Generating Positive Changes

Looking at the lower animals, we can see that even though their activities are extremely simple, almost all of their activities initiate efforts to promote their survival, i.e., they create *positive changes* for them. Most of these activities are built around three basic functions - eating, mating and protecting their territories. The first two acts create the *positive changes* directly by supporting their survival efforts, and deliver pleasures to the animals directly, while the third act enables them to perform the first two acts. It is obvious that the animals are attracted to those activities by the pleasures they deliver, and so they keep on repeating those acts, hoping for more. And, since most of their acts generate *positive changes,* the lower animals seem to stay in sync with the cosmic *force field of life* quite faithfully.

The most obvious difference between the activities of the human and those of the lower animals is, of course, in the amounts and the intensities of the *positive change*. Using advanced intelligence, human activities are generating many times more *positive changes* than the lower animals. We are at the highest level on the evolutionary ladder on this planet probably because we are promoting evolution with the highest amount of *positive changes.* The speed of evolution has increased significantly since the appearance of man, and has taken off exponentially the last few hundred years or so. But there is also a dark side. Along with huge amounts of *positive changes,* human activities are also producing significantly high amounts of *negative changes,* while the lower animals create almost no *negative changes.* This is a significant difference between man and lower animals, which may suggest that man may be falling out of the right track of evolution. Some of our *negative changes* are appearing as destructive acts, and are accumulating on our planet creating serious threats to our survival in the far future. They are affecting the nature of our evolution adversely. Pollution, overpopulation, the climate change, etc. are some of the results that are posing serious threats to our well being and survival in the future.

Our activities are creating a mix of *positive* and *negative changes,* and from all the destructive activities that we have accumulated, it seems that the ratio of the *negative* to the *positive changes* is much higher with us than with the lower animals. And, this may be a significant and unique feature of the human evolution. It appears that at the lower levels of evolutionary ladder, the creatures show a much less vigorous but a purer form of evolution, while at a much higher level, the human evolution is many times more powerful, but probably distorted!

A general flowchart for evolution for all life forms may look like:

*Pursuit of Happiness --> Activity ---> positive and negative changes --->
net change(=positive changes offset by negative changes) ---> Survive &
Evolve(if positive)*

The lower animals create almost no *negative changes.* Thus, even if their production of *positive changes* is low compared to that of the humans, the *net change* created by the lower animals is always *positive*. We, on the other hand, create significant amounts of *negative changes*; thus the net change for us may not be *positive* all the time. Consequently, we can see that serious amounts of destructive acts are piling up and sounding alarms for us. The *global warming* may be one prime example. Our negative acts effectively diminish our overall positivity, and since the speed of our evolution is proportional to the rate of our production of *positive changes,* they adversely affect the speed of our evolution by reducing the net *positive change*.

It's the overall change, taking into account many changes

As mentioned above, we produce a mix of *positive* and *negative changes* through most of our activities. Thus, over a period of time, there is a net or over all status change created by our activities, which, according to our theory, will be significant in influencing the nature of the outcome - whether it will increase the likelihood of happiness or the probability of misery by being in sync or out of sync with the cosmic *force field of life.*

It is possible that a status change can bring happiness to a person while causing misery to others; i.e., a *positive change* for the self can be a *negative change* for some others. This can lead to conflicts and destructive activities, and can create overall *negative changes*, slowing down our evolution by waste of energy through endless infighting. But, it seems that Nature(the cosmic *force field of life)* has programmed a sense in living beings, so that we recognize a *true positive change* as one that promotes the preservation and evolution of life. Thus, a true *positive change* is instinctively sensed by a normal[1] person as an over all positive status change, taking into account many individual status changes in many areas, not just considering only the status change that benefits the person himself.

Thus, a true *positive change* for me should include, for example, *positive changes* in my world, as well as in the worlds of my immediate family, relatives, friends, community, my country, and this planet, all graduated on a scale of varying importance levels. So, for example, on a scale of 10(10 being the highest), the importance levels of the different components mentioned above for a normal person would be like:

my interests: 7
my immediate family's interests: 6
my relatives' interests: 5
my friends' interests: 4
my community's interests: 3
my country's interests: 2
the world's interests: 1

On the other hand, a person having a sociopathic tendency may rank the importance levels of the same elements differently. For example, he may rank them as:

my interests: 10
my immediate family's interests: 5
my relatives' interests: 2
my friends' interests: 2
my community's interests: 0
my country's interests: 0
the world's interests: 0

At the other extreme, for example, a monk may rank the elements in this way:

my interests: 1
my immediate family's interests: 8
my relatives' interests: 8

my friends' interests: 8
my community's interests: 8
my country's interests: 8
the world's interests: 8

The concept of the *positive change* may differ to a degree from person to person, as the priority levels of the different elements may be slightly different, but for all normal people[1] (defined as approximately average in any psychological trait, as intelligence, personality, or emotional adjustment), this difference is expected to stay within a narrow range. Thus, even with all our individual differences, our individual over all *energy field* is roughly in sync with the cosmic *force field of life*, and is promoting the process of evolution. In the theoretical case, if people having sociopathic tendencies outnumber normal people, we fall out of sync, moving towards extinction through lack of unity and destructive fights.

We probably also can define a 'normal person' in this light. We can describe the person as one, whose character traits keep his/her *energy field* in sync with the cosmic *force field of life*. The regular everyday activities of the person would produce both *positive* and *negative changes*, but the *positive* activities would outnumber negative ones, so that the net *change* created by the person would be positive. This would support and promote the process of evolution, and the person would qualify to receive different types of happiness of living as rewards. But this 'normalcy' can be vulnerable to many elements of living in the systems of the society, and abnormality may creep in.

An Important Question:

The question is, 'Is it okay to get involved in the activities that create *positive changes* for me but negative changes for others?' This is a very common, natural question. So, let's analyze it a bit.

Let's consider the case of Sam, who is an average man, with wife and two kids.

He also has 5 close relatives, 6 close friends, 3 competitors or enemies, and that he lives in a community of about 10,000 people. A net *positive change* for Sam will include *positive changes* in Sam's personal status, as well as in the statuses of his immediate family, his relatives, his friends, his community, his country, and the world, in varying priorities or importance levels, graduated on a scale of 10.

Sam, for example, may rank the priorities of the different possible *positive changes* in the following way:

*Positive change*s for	Priority Level
Sam himself:	7
Sam's competitor/enemy:	0
Sam's immediate family:	6
Sam's close friends:	5
Sam's close relatives:	4
Sam's community:	2
Sam's country:	1
the world:	0.01

Since Sam is an average normal person, his acts are naturally biased to benefit himself and his close circles more than others. But a normal average person also cares for the well being of his larger circles involving his community, his country and finally the world - even though with progressively less priorities. Then, let's look at the resulting respective priority scores.

The Priority Scores for the different circles:

Sam's total priority score =
priority score given by Sam himself + score from his immediate family members + score from his close relatives + score from his friends + score from his community + score from his country + score from the rest of the world.

Sam's priority score from himself = 7.

Sam's priority score from competitors(enemies) = 3x0 = 0.

Assuming Sam's family members, relatives and friends have priority structures similar to those of Sam(since Sam is assumed to be an average normal person):

Sam's immediate family members' contribution to his priority score:

   Three family members each giving a score of 6 to Sam,
   the family members' score towards Sam's priority = 6x3 = 18.

c)   Six close friends, each giving a score of 5,
   the friends' contribution towards Sam's priority = 6x5 = 30.

c)   Five close relatives, each giving a score of 4,
   the relatives' contribution towards Sam's priority = 4x5 = 20.

The community, the country and the rest of the world don't practice any preferential treatments; thus they don't contribute anything to Sam's priority score. But normally, everybody contribute to the priority scores of the community, the country and the world, as was shown in the above priority table.

Thus, Sam's total priority score = 7+18+30+20 = 75

If the community's population is 10,000, then each person contributing 2 priority points, the total priority score for the community = 2x10000 = 20,000

Similarly, if the country's population is 300,000000, then
the country's total priority score = 1x300000000 = 300,000,000

And, with a population of 7.5 billion,
The priority score for the world = 0.01x7500000000 = 75,000,000

The above example shows that the priority scores of Sam's community, his country and the world are much higher than his own score, which means that even if the average normal person gets active in the pursuit of his/her own success(happiness), the person would create a positive environment in his/her greater worlds promoting the creation of *positive changes* by them.

The above illustration also shows that it is justified for someone to create *positive changes* benefiting himself and his close circles, even if they harm(generate *negative changes*) to his competitors or enemies - as long as the person's activities create *positive changes* for the greater world around the person, e.g., his community, his country and the world, even with much less priorities. Actually, this kind of activities promotes competition, and helps find the leaders in different areas of activities.

As a byproduct of this discussion, we may have found a very important feature for a 'normal person'. Being a product of the cosmic *force field of life*, a normal person is expected to promote the function of the force field, which is to promote the evolution of life. A normal person accomplishes this by creating an environment conducive for the creation of *positive changes* by all. Thus, a normal person, in addition to caring for himself and his/her inner circles, cares for others in his/her bigger worlds helping them can create their *positive changes*. And, it is also normal that this concern for the greater worlds is much milder than the concern for his/her own closer circles.

Chapter Ten

The Importance of Activities in Human Evolution

It is quite possible that Ray the plumber who came to fix your leaky faucet last time, could have been a Math wizard if he didn't drop out of school early in his life, and pursued higher education! He probably could have been able to detect and utilize his hidden talent, and attained a high level of proficiency on the subject. Perhaps, then he could have created some *positive changes* in the world around with his contributions and promoted human evolution. And, chances are high that there are many 'Ray's in our societies who never get discovered, because they don't get involved or can't afford to get involved in the appropriate educational activities to detect and develop their hidden talents. Thus, it is quite likely that only a small fraction of available human intellectual potential is being utilized to promote human evolution!

It appears that as evolution reaches higher levels, it becomes progressively more difficult to detect the potentially beneficial biological changes, and then select the appropriate activities to utilize them to create *positive changes*. In today's highly evolved human, those *changes* are extremely minute and subtle. Also, most of them are happening inside our brain, and thus they are mostly undetectable without the use of an extensive and well planned set of activities, which generally come in the forms of different educational programs. Sometimes a gifted child may find an aptitude in a certain direction early, but then dramatically change course later in life and finds the subject of real passion! It seems that the human mind matures through many bends and valleys before finding its true course. A close friend of mine has been a technology professional all her life, and has a doctorate degree in her subject. A few years ago she took early retirement to follow her true passion of writing poetry and literature, and has earned many accolades since then. Thus, it can be a truly difficult task to recognize a human intellectual talent and then utilize it with the right activity. This may also mean that we should stay prepared to use an extensive routine of diverse educational activities in order to recognize and utilize our intellectual talents effectively.

The lower animals normally don't have to go through a difficult process of detecting the potentially beneficial status *changes* happening through biological changes. Because the beneficial *changes* are mostly physical and obvious, and generally happen in the areas of eating, mating and protecting its territory, where physical superiority is most useful. The creatures detect and utilize those beneficial changes through a short list of basic activities consisting mainly of eating, mating and protecting territory. So, the appropriate activity is selected quickly, and the status *changes* are converted into *positive changes* to promote their survival quite easily.

As we have discussed before:

$$Positive\ Change => status\ change \times Appropriate\ Activity$$

Where the symbol '=>' is used to mean 'depends upon'

And, since the survival of a species is directly proportional to the amount of *positive changes* happening in its evolutionary path,

Evolution => Positive Changes => status changes x Appropriate Activity

In the absence of any external overriding factor,

Evolution => Positive Changes => Biological Changes x Appropriate Activity

Thus, biological changes and the appropriate activities to detect and utilize them seem to be the two most important factors in the evolution of life forms. The creatures don't seem to have any control on the first factor, but they may be able to control the second one. It seems that in the path of evolution of the life forms, from the lowly amoeba to today's man, the beneficial biological changes have gradually changed from predominantly physical to predominantly intellectual in nature, and also from mostly visible to mostly hidden.

Different Types of status changes

Going back at the topic of *status changes,* we can see that of both, the *positive* and *negative* status changes or simply the *positive* and the *negative changes* are happening continuously in our world, and in the world around us. Some are happening due to factors beyond our control, and some are caused by our activities. The *changes* which are caused by our acts are the ones which we can control, and make them *positive* or *negative*. For example, using good nutrition and taking part in physical workouts, we can create *positive changes* by creating better health, which is an important factor affecting our future happiness. Providing nurture to a child in need is another example of a different type of act that creates *positive changes*. The child gets a *positive change* in his/her status through the psychological and other practical supports, while the provider gets the *positive change* for psychological reasons. The act helps the provider to stay in sync with the *force field of life* because of promoting the well being of the child. And, the *positive changes* generated by the act can deliver happiness to both.

And, like all other life forms, we seem to know instinctively what is a *positive* for us and what is *negative,* and we naturally lean towards the *positive.* This, of course, seems only natural, because being a product of the *force field of life*, we would naturally like to get and stay in sync with this master cosmic *force field of life* by creating or promoting *positive changes,* since the *force field of life* is the source of all positivity. Our brain seems to have the capability to examine all the happenings around us, and tag them as *positive* or *negative* with their different intensities. This mechanism is instinctive, but most of the times we override it with our advanced intelligence in most of our activities.

There are numerous examples of our everyday activities around us that are either creating *positive* or *negative changes* or a combination of the two. The nature of some are quite obvious, and some are very subtle. An average person's typical daily activities may consist of some *positive* acts, and some *negative* acts, and over a period of time there is a net or overall quality, which is *positive* or *negative* in nature. Our theory says, the more a person is overall *positive*, the more is his/her chances of finding happiness, because the *positive changes* increase the degree of sync with the cosmic *force field of life.* The person with a well-tuned mind is generally more efficient in controlling his/her activities to find happiness. The constant eagerness to create *positive changes* probably increases the sensitivity of the mind to feel or detect a *positive change* more efficiently. Thus perhaps, the mere attitude created by this constant *positive* urge changes the chemistry of the mind gradually, and at a certain level the mind is able to find many subtle and fragile sources of happiness that it didn't know existed before. Perhaps, this is the state where the mind finds true *serenity!* Perhaps, this is a state of mind that is attained through the practice of *Jnana Yoga* on the journey to *Moksha*, as mentioned in the Bhagavad-Gita[24].

It is obvious that like most other animals, we also use the acts of eating and mating to create *positive changes* of the most basic and yet the most important types, and get rewarded with pleasures and happiness. But in addition, with the help of our advanced intelligence, we create many other activities to find happiness. They appear in many different forms and shades, from the most simple to the extremely complex ones, through a multitude of activities which create *positive* and/or *negative changes* directly or indirectly.

But with the advanced intelligence, we also have found a *shortcut* to happiness using activities which generally create little or no *positive changes*. These are our items of *pleasure*, which can be considered as a subset of the larger category of Happiness. According to modern psychology, they generally belong to the hedonistic[48,49] type of happiness. The question may arise in our mind that since these activities do not create *positive changes*, how do they generate any form of happiness at all! The answer may lie in the fact that a pleasure is not a true happiness. They may be the fringe benefits of the conducive environment created by *positive changes*. Many of these items of pleasure are obtainable only when our survival and safety are assured by other true *positive changes*.

Also, sometimes a *major positive change* becomes a *minor* one when its importance decreases because of changes in the environment or the situation. For example, normally the acts of eating and mating can produce huge amounts of *positive changes*. But, in the early days of the humans, when they were not having problems finding food or mate, they were fighting for their survival against the powerful animals. Many of these animals were physically stronger than them, and so a direct physical fight would have led to a convincing loss for the humans. But their superior intelligence came to the rescue.

They were able to amplify their physical capabilities by inventing tools. This created the vital *positive changes* for them which helped them win their fight and survive. The activities of eating and mating were still producing *positive changes,* but they were not furnishing the emergency needs. the survival was not threatened because of lack of food or mates. Their advanced intelligence was more important for their survival; and since then has been creating more *positive changes* for the humans than the acts of just eating and mating. Now, even if those acts are not crucial for pushing the frontier of evolution, they have become big producers of the type of happiness called pleasure. But, if people are not careful, these acts of pleasure can create even *negative changes* in the form of problems created by overpopulation, overeating or eating bad food just for taste!

Thus, as we evolve, our world or environment changes, and we face different types of challenges. Then, new activities are needed to create new types of *positive changes,* perhaps in different areas to assure our survival. And, at present it seems that we are entering a new era when we are beginning to learn more about our real neighborhood, the universe and the new challenges to survive there.

As we discussed earlier, *positive changes* for a species are created when status changes are utilized by them using appropriate activities, making them beneficial for their survival. In the earlier stages of human evolution, the beneficial *changes* were obvious, and the right activities were chosen almost automatically. Also, there was an urgency to find the right activities, as survival was at stake. The early humans were competing against physically stronger animals. So, they focused on the most obvious status changes having the potential of becoming *positive changes and* help their survival efforts. The most important *status change*s were happening in their brain, which gave them superior intelligence. They quickly realized that they couldn't win against the stronger animals in bare, one to one physical fights; and needed some extra help. Their superior intelligence found a solution, with the invention and the use of tools, which gave them additional help by amplifying their capabilities. The 'tools' gave the humans a clear edge over other animals in the competition for survival, and created a huge *positive change* for them. Thus, here the right activities(use of intelligence) used a status change(superior brain) to create *positive changes* which increased the survival capabilities of the humans.

As we have been moving up the ladder of evolution, Nature (the cosmic *force field of life*) most probably has been giving us a string of biological *changes*, which could have been random or triggered by some environmental factors. Some of those *changes* were utilized and converted to *positive changes* by the appropriate activities, and the unused ones faded out with time, contributing towards no survival advantages. Probably most of the useful beneficial *changes* have been occurring in our area of intelligence, and we have been using new and innovative activities to convert them to *positive changes*. But, it is quite possible that so far we have used only a small portion of all the potentially beneficial *physical changes* that may have already accumulated in our brain, and we need to find ingenious ways to utilize them!

As life kept on moving up the evolutionary ladder, the list of capabilities and activities kept on increasing creating new *positive changes*. With the humans, the activities have been expanded enormously to take advantage of the possible continuous evolution of the brain. Most of the beneficial *changes* happening there have been subtle and unpredictable. Also, it is quite difficult to detect their presence from the regular behavior of the human child. As we moved up the ladder of evolution, it is getting progressively more difficult to detect the presence of the potentially beneficial *biological changes* that may have been happening in the human brain, and then use the appropriate acts to convert them to *positive changes*. Thus, it is quite feasible that there have been numerous cases where a person's talents(*beneficial changes*) have never been discovered because of the lack of use of the proper activities. Therefore, a comprehensive program of activities covering all the bases may be urgently needed by the human civilization for utilizing all the potential talents that may be happening to the human race through evolution.

On the other side, the *force field of life* created by the immense cosmic energy is perhaps inducing the beneficial *biological changes* in a steady stream in life forms that promote evolution! Even if they have been occurring gradually at a seemingly very slow pace, we probably have not been able to keep pace with them by utilizing them to create *positive changes* with the proper activities. Thus, they may have been collecting in our brain, and have been accumulating with time! Thus, perhaps the saying, 'we only use a small fraction of our brain's capabilities' is an accurate statement! It's like, while doing some exploration of vast unexplored territories, we construct a road, and then use it to go further into the territory. Our subsequent exploration is influenced by the location of this first road. Then further construction of the side roads will also be in the vicinity of the first road, while vast territories still lie unexplored, out of reach of the roads. We need many more roads. Our activities to find and utilize our beneficial *changes* are probably like constructing those roads - they are influenced and limited by the existing cultural and other human factors. It may be extremely difficult to discover and utilize all the beneficial *changes* that may be happening in our brain. This also implies that, if appropriate activities are chosen, even an average person may be able to produce a lot more *positive changes* than otherwise.

Thus, for us, the humans, it seems vitally important to explore a multitude of different activities including various educational and training programs so that we are able to find the appropriate activities to utilize our hidden talents. Consequently, human evolution depends upon the nature of our activities to create *positive changes*, and the more people can contribute, the stronger will be the evolution. But unfortunately, there are some formidable roadblocks, of which the socioeconomic factors are probably the biggest ones. We wonder what would have happened to the life story of Albert Einstein, if he were born in one of the poverty-stricken, underdeveloped parts of the world! And, chances are high that there have been many other 'Einstein's in our civilization, who never got a chance to use their talents, and faded away!

Then, there are the taboos, prejudices and superstitions that restrict the production of *positive changes* by following the wrong path of beliefs. Restrictive political climates can also affect the generation of *positive changes* adversely. This probably happens typically when wrong leaders are elected who lack the attitude and foresight to encourage activities that create *positive changes* for the human race and bring prosperity to the people. Another big flaw in our civilization may be the concept of 'profit' which is translated only through monetary terms.

Looking at our past, we see tremendous innovations. But those innovations have not improved our chances of survival as a human species as much as they have created problems, which are accumulating fast and are sounding alarms for our future well being! Probably, one of the main reasons why this happens is that we have devised a system in our civilization where most of our ventures are motivated by monetary profits, which are achieved quite often by harming other valuable things of life. Thus our businesses are deciding our future, and we may not be following the right path of life promoting the *positive changes* and evolution. We need a true cultural revolution, so that our thought processing gets changed, and we are are guided by true profits, not just monetary profits. A *true profit* should be a sum of many types of profits which should create overall *positive changes* in our world, promoting evolution and consequently our survival as a species in the universe - perhaps, even beyond this planet. But this cultural change needs to be instilled in our minds early in our lives through education in our schools as early as possible.

The evolution of the mind

Recently we were playing the Bridge game while the TV was on. In between programs, an ad came up, talking about some upcoming *spiritual* gathering. In the ad some clips of a video were being shown, in which a spiritual person was answering some questions of the audience. My skeptic mind rose quickly and wanted not to pay any attention to it! But then I decided to give it a few seconds of my time and kept on listening to him while playing Bridge at the same time. But the question and his answer grabbed my attention! The question to him basically was, why there is so much suffering in the world today in spite of all the advancements in science and technology! The Yogi replied, it is because the inner soul of man has not improved much, only his activities have expanded.

The answer made me take a pause in the middle of my game - it sounded so right! I realized the hard truth behind the comment. It also satisfied our theory of *positive change*. It is true that our activities have expanded by leaps and bounds through the tremendous advancements in Arts, Sciences, and the Technologies, but the amount of miseries and struggles around don't seem to have gone down! Perhaps, this is because we are not using those advanced tools to produce a large amount of *positive changes* to promote our evolution and our survival. The evolutionary capabilities are generally defined in terms of the abilities to survive. We may not be using the right activities that would optimally utilize our beneficial biological changes that may have been happening inside our brains! We are just staying satisfied acquiring mostly the *easy pleasures* of life like the low hanging fruits of a tree, and not trying for the true *happiness* that requires an effort for creating or promoting the *positive changes*!

On our time scale the evolution of mind may appear to be happening extremely slowly. Around 250 BC, King Ashoka gave up his throne after winning the big war at Kalinga in India, and became a monk. He had the power of his kingdom and the opportunity to enjoy all the materialistic pleasures of life, but he gave them all up, and started preaching love, peace and spirituality. His efforts helped to spread the great religion of Buddhism in the world. This has been a great milestone for the evolution of the mind which has produced an enormous amount of *positive changes*. We probably have not passed that milestone yet while about 2270 years have passed since! Our theory says, love and peace create the perfect medium for the production of *positive changes*. Thus, they help people stay in sync with the cosmic *force field of life* leading to the prosperity and evolution.

Nonetheless, we probably are sitting on a good storage of beneficial *changes* already in our brain. Now, the challenge to us is to find and get involved in the right kind of activities that would utilize and convert them to *positive changes*. We do have the benchmark educational programs in our cultural systems, but they probably need to be updated continuously with new ideas to detect newer types of potential beneficial changes that may be happening within us. This probably means that we need to develop a constant attitude of pursuing the *positive change*, and not stay satisfied with just the materialistic pleasures. Here our mind probably can play an important role, so that we can develop an instinct of leaning towards the right direction to seek and promote the *positive changes*. Perhaps, this would keep the human race on the path of enlightenment striving to find the maximum possible sync with the cosmic *force field of life*.

Chapter Eleven

Some Random Thoughts

Our *theory* says that a stable and lasting foundation of happiness is built by creating or promoting *positive changes* through our physical and mental activities. This requires that those activities promote not only our own personal well being, but also the well being of the greater world around us. Thus it confirms our age old wisdom flowing through the generations of human civilization. The status changes created by these activities are true *positive changes*. And, since by definition a *positive change* promotes the survival of the species, the activities that create *positive changes* and consequently deliver us happiness are linked with the survival of our species. Also, this is how we stay in sync with the master *force field of life* shrouding our planet. Now we can see a clear flow-chart of life on our planet. Activities that promote their survival, generate *positive changes* and deliver happiness(pleasure). The life forms are attracted to these activities because of the pleasure, and keep on repeating them until a beneficial physical change happens, most probably by random chance, which increases the capabilities of the life form and lifts it to the next higher level of evolution. And this goes on for all life forms on this planet which has created the human species, starting from the lowly amoebas. This seems to be the way the supreme cosmic energy shrouding our planet is creating higher evolution of life here.

Thus, it seems that it is important to always look at the *big picture* while planning our activities in the pursuit of our personal happiness. According to our theory as explained, this is accomplished by activities that create *positive changes*. They promote the survival of our species. And, since survival is directly proportional to evolution, our positive acts in the pursuit of happiness promote our evolution. Most of our successful activities accomplish this requirement in humdrum ways, using our common sense without making us aware of their deeper significance. For example, eating food makes us stay alive, and the act also promotes our survival as the human species. And, it brings pleasure, and pleasure is a form of happiness. Reproductive activities also work the same way using the same principle but uses different type of activities. The nature of the majority of our activities are generally instinctively known to us, and our theory agrees with the general consensus but uses a different method. Our theory accomplishes this by checking to see whether the activities produce an overall *positive change* or not. For example, it is well recognized that overpopulation is a negative act, because it is detrimental to our well being. Our theory agrees because it creates *negative changes* by restricting the availability of the basic needs to many. Similarly, our activities that generate pollution are also creating *negative changes*, because pollution adversely affects our environment on which we depend for our life and health.

But, there are other times when the situation is complicated with too many variables, and our common sense or instinct alone may not be able to help us decide the proper course of action. Here the possibilities of mistakes increase, and we may fail to select the appropriate activities in our pursuit of happiness. This type of situation often leads to the generation of destructive activities, which accumulate with time as we can see all around us on our planet. They are increasing fast and creating serious problems on our path of survival and evolution! There are many activities which are difficult to classify as positive or negative. Here our formula of *positive change* can be helpful in selecting the right activities. For example, it may be difficult to rate the activities inspired by *greed* on a constant basis. *Greed* often has two sides. On one hand it initiates acts that promote prosperity through innovations and discoveries that create jobs and livelihood for people. Significant amounts of *positive changes* can be created through these activities. On the other hand, we also see acts of greed creating positive status change only for a few while harming many, creating overall *negative change* for our species. Thus, here a check for the overall status change may reveal a *negative change*. Thus, a check for the overall status change may be an important test, which may give us an indication whether we are selecting the proper activities in the different situations of life. And, we have a natural ability to detect a *positive change* - its practice may make us more efficient in using it. The unique requirement of a true *positive change* is that it promotes the well being of the self as well as that of the greater world around. Sometimes the latter one can be extremely minute and subtle, and should not be ignored, otherwise we may create *negative changes,* which may lead to destructive acts.

Everyday regular activities can have a direct link with our happiness through the creation of *positive changes*. These acts may be physical, mental, or a combination of the two, and most of the times the activity creating the *positive change* is very simple, and the amount of the *positive change* created is extremely miniscule. It may be as simple as hugging our kids, or following proper eating habits, and so on. The act of hugging our kids helps to create a nurturing environment that encourages growth and prosperity in many unique ways. The habit of eating right helps to keep ourselves healthy and capable of creating *positive changes*. Thus, both are *positive* acts. As we strive to create *positive changes* consistently through our activities, our attitude can change altering the chemistry of our mind. Its eagerness and sensitivity may rise to increase its efficiency for creating and promoting positivity. Thus, in our pursuit of happiness, the presence of the right attitude seems to be truly important. If we define *positive* acts as the activities that create *positive changes*, the types of *positive* acts are increasing exponentially to utilize the beneficial physical changes that may have been happening in our areas of intelligence. We have explored this subject in more details later, in the chapter titled, *the positive change*.

As mentioned before, our happiness or the well being seems to depend on our degree of sync with the cosmic master *force field of life* shrouding our planet, which in turn depends upon the *positive changes* created by our activities. A higher degree of sync not only creates deeper base of happiness, but also help us evolve faster developing newer capabilities because of wasting less energy in counter-productive activities. But, quite often it may be difficult to realize our degree of sync with the *force field of life* from the humdrum nature of our daily activities. Generally, we have the instinctive sense to detect the *positive acts* from the *negative* ones, and it helps us to stay in sync. Numerous daily activities fall in this category. In these situations, we can check to see if collectively they are producing a net *positive* or a net *negative* change in the world around us. For example, let's take a look at our simple act of cleaning our house. The act helps us reduce clutter and store things in their proper places, enabling us to find our needed tools and stuff more quickly and easily. Thus, it helps us to increase our efficiency so that we can take part in other *positive* activities. Thus, the act creates a *positive change* in our living status by enabling us to accomplish more in a certain amount of time. Also, cleaning our room may help us to reduce any harmful germ and insects, if present, creating further *positive changes* in our status. Therefore, the activity is net *positive*, and links with the possibility of happiness.

But, at the same time, we have to realize that we can't assume that all cleanliness minded people are happy, because cleaning the room may be just one of hundreds of other acts over a certain period of time, which create status changes of their own, and it is the overall *change* that should matter. In general, we get involved in groups of activities in which some are *positive*, some *negative*, all probably with different intensities and the overall or the net change may be *positive* or *negative*. Over a period of time, say a week or so, we can be net *positive* or net *negative*. Logically, our happiness depends on the degree of net positivity. This net *change* over a longer period is important, because it probably gives us an indication about the *happiness profile* of the person, i.e., the natural tendency of the person to lean towards happiness.

At the earlier, lower levels of evolution, where advanced intelligence is not developed significantly in creatures yet, the activities to create *positive changes* are simple and predominantly physical. Eating, mating and protecting one's territory make up the majority of their activities. Most of those acts create *positive changes* directly for them as they help them survive. As evolution started reaching higher levels, the advancing intelligence started playing increasingly more important roles in composing their activities, which started to become progressively more complex. At present, with the humans, the mind is playing the most vital role in designing their activities that create most of the *positive changes*. Thus, for us, some of our most effective acts are purely mental. The acts of love and affection, for example, are among the most powerful generators of *positive changes* and happiness for us.

The *positive* acts contribute to create an overall conducive environment for the creation of *positive changes* by others, and reward all of us with an environment of happiness and cooperation. Helping the children by getting involved in their lives seems to be one of the most productive *positive* acts. Because the children, when given the opportunity to grow properly, have high potential of creating huge amounts of *positive changes* in the world around. This is specially true with the young people who are having difficulty in finding enough support to grow right. In the older ages, when the physical abilities start to decline, the easier sources of happiness start to dwindle. Then, we may need to be creative in creating *positive changes* through somewhat passive but effective ways which may not require our direct physical involvement as much.

Since happiness depends upon the creation of *positive* status changes, finding *happiness* is not limited to the materialistic ways only. Material wealth can help people generate *positive changes* at earlier stages of growth by meeting or exceeding the basic necessities for survival and well being, but beyond that stage the surplus wealth may not be able to generate much additional *positive changes*. The wealth itself does not create *positive changes* - their creation depends upon the nature of the activities of the person having the wealth. Different types of *positive* activities are needed for that purpose which in turn depends upon the attitude of the person. Thus, though it is logical to think that access to wealth may make it easier to create *positive changes*, in reality this may not be the case. Often, along with the wealth come many corrupting elements that affect the mind of the person, changing its chemistry adversely. The theory here provides a logical support to the often-heard wisdom that we don't need a lot of material wealth to find happiness; even though, probably very few have real conviction in it!

The knowledge that our happiness does not depend on material wealth can have a deep implication. It can make our mind free - free to choose the area of activities of life where we would like to create *positive changes,* not just follow the track of money. Not everybody can be wealthy - even if the person is talented and is contributing to the society by creating *positive changes*. Getting wealthy depends upon many factors controlled by the systems of the society, many of which may not have been created with fairness in mind. But happiness is probably known as the ultimate prize of life - it is the driver of all activities of life. It should be accessible to everybody, who is creating *positive changes*. And, our theory says, it is; although the factor of difficulty may vary from person to person. This wisdom encourages us to pursue the profession of our choice with passion, irrespective of its money making prospects, leading to explorations and innovations in all directions promoting evolution. Thus, it may be extremely useful to realize and always remember that we have unlimited potential to find happiness even when we may not find wealth.

We pursue happiness in many different ways, but many of those efforts don't succeed. It is very likely that our unsuccessful efforts generate overall *negative changes*, making us out of sync with the master *force field of life*, thus increasing the possibilities of misery. This can happen even when the short term effect of the act may be *positive* but the longer term effect is *negative*. This can also happen when the activity benefits a few, but harms many. Perhaps, our theory can explain why it is possible for the middle-income teacher to be happier than the wealthy business owner, for example. Generally, the teacher has many more options available in his profession to promote *positive changes* than the business owner. Guiding the young lives on the right path of life can generate a tremendous amount of *positive changes*. On the other hand, generally a businessman is always looking to make a materialistic profit for himself, and perhaps, there is a natural tendency or temptation to make a profit even at the cost of the well being of others. impacting others negatively. Thus, there is the possibility of the creation of an overall *negative change*.

One of the most common causes of misery probably occurs the same way when we try to find our happiness at the expense of others! Here, the *positive changes* created by the activities are offset by the *negative changes* done to the people around, and the over all *change* becomes *negative*. The 'neighbor's yard is greener' syndrome is also created in a similar way. This may happen when we fail to focus on our own 'blessings'. Most of the times, we generally have multiple sources at our disposal, with which we could create our own *positive changes*, and strengthen our base of happiness. They may not be happening in the forms of big materialistic gains or obviously *positive status changes,* but may be simple and subtle elements that are effective in creating reliable *positive changes.* But often we fail to utilize them, and keep on looking at others peoples' happiness in a jealous way. Probably, many criminal behaviors are started using the same mechanism.

The theory also explains why it is unwise to have blind obsessions. Often, in our pursuit of happiness, we fall in love with a particular activity that has been producing happiness for us reliably for a quite a long time. Gradually, it becomes our main reliable source of happiness, and we probably close our mind to other possible sources of happiness. Thus we get obsessed with this activity. without realizing that we love the act because of the *positive changes* it produces. But things can change when the act may fail to accomplish it, and stop being a source of happiness. Thus, our theory suggests to keep our mind open and active, and open for other activities that create *positive changes.*

One important variable in our equation of happiness may be the nature of the environment in which we all live. A friendly environment can make it easier to create *positive changes* than in a uncooperative or hostile environment. Love, in its many different forms encourages growth and prosperity of life. It appears that the environment created by love of various types is the ideal medium that encourages creation of *positive changes* through the right activities. In turn, they help us stay in sync with the *force field of life,* and promote evolution. Thus, with everything else same, the person having a friendly or affectionate disposition, may be able to create the environment for generation of *positive changes* more effortlessly than others.

In our lives, we are surrounded by many faint and fragile sources of happiness - we fail to capture many of them, and thus reduce the efficiency of our mind. If we become aware of the role of the simple *positive change* in finding happiness, we probably would become a lot happier human race! I remember an old friend of many years ago, who used find happiness by watching the leaves of his plants grow! He was raising some plants in pots. Every morning, he used to come by the plants, water, and sit next to them for a while. He told me that he used to find a serene happiness just watching them grow. We think, we can increase our mind's efficiency of finding happiness by increasing its sensitivity of detecting the simple and mild *positive changes*. A sustained practice may be able achieve this. A highly tuned mind would be continually striving to create *positive changes* through all its daily activities automatically, effortlessly. And, in doing so, we would also bring our mind in sync with the master *force field of life*, which may be the scientific reason for happiness.

The nature of our personal energy is expressed through our mental and physical activities. Like a vector quantity, it can be in sync or out of sync with the *force field of life* in varying degrees, generating corresponding reactions. It seems that we have one very special capability, which is generally not found in other animals, who are even slightly lower than us in the evolutionary rank. It is our ability to act against the *force field of life* through behaviors that resist or oppose the trend of evolution through the creation of *negative changes*. We often cause this by favoring short term personal gains of a few, ignoring long term benefits of the masses. A business person trying to make monetary profit by selling a product harmful to others, or a politician pushing for harmful changes in the laws of the country for personal gains, are some of the examples of this behavior. It seems that we also behave this way when we get misguided by emotions like anger, jealousy and so on. Then our activities create *negative changes,* and make us out of sync with the *force field of life* increasing the possibilities of misery.

But those same emotions are also products of the advanced brain, and thus are the results of higher evolution! Therefore, most probably, there is a hidden purpose for their presence here. Perhaps, it is that those same mental attributes can also speed up the generation of *positive changes,* and thus raise the speed of our evolution when used properly. Thus, it seems that it is important how we use our emotions properly - by making sure the end product is an overall *positive change.*

The intensity of interaction between our individual personal energies and the master *force field of life* is probably extremely mild, but the effect can be multiplied a million times by millions of people taking part in similar type of activities like atoms in a large mass. It can accumulate over time to significant amounts, and may create the ambience of our environment of living, which probably influence the abundance of our happiness or the frequency of our miseries on this planet. The progress of human civilization may be happening in small steps of *positive changes* contributed by many; and they accumulate into huge amounts; but we are also creating destructive acts at an alarming pace. As a result, it is not easy to say confidently if we are creating a net *positive change* through our activities. We probably have more capabilities to speed up our evolution, but perhaps we aren't choosing the right activities.

Chapter Twelve

Different Types of Happiness - The Secondary Sources

As explained before, the activities in the pursuit of happiness can produce different types of status changes in our personal world and in the world around. The status changes that appear *positive* or beneficial to us, seem to deliver us happiness. But some of these status changes may or may not be *positive* or beneficial for the greater world around. To the contrary, some of them may actually produce harmful effects or *negative* status changes for the world around. Thus, the status changes can be divided into two main types according to the nature of its effects on the *self* and on the greater world around:

1) *Positive* for the *self*, and also *positive* for the world around.

2) *Positive* for the *self*, and immaterial for the world around.

self meaning the person creating the activities and his/her close circle of people.

The first type of status changes are the true *positive changes*. According to our theory they constitute the primary sources of happiness that create a strong foundation through activities that benefit both the *self* and the world around. As explained before, these activities help us stay in sync with the *force field of life* by generating *positive changes*. This type of happiness has been classified as the eudaimonic[48,49] type of happiness by modern psychology. Generally, the activities in the pursuit of this type of happiness try to uplift not only the status of the person creating it, but also the overall status of the greater world around making the status changes true *positive changes*. These are produced by many different kinds of activities ranging from the dramatic *positive* acts to the everyday regular humdrum activities. They can be physical and/or mental. Nothing spectacular is required - just the attitude to create a *positive* ending in whatever we are doing is probably the most important variable in the equation of the *positive change*. The next step is to support this attitude with our efforts - whatever effort can be applied comfortably is adequate most of the times.

The second type of status changes make up the secondary sources of happiness, commonly known as the *pleasures*. According to modern psychology, they are known as the hedonistic[48,49] sources of happiness. The main focus of this type of happiness is self-gratification without much concern for the greater world around. They are generated from activities that produces effects, which are beneficial for the *self*, without considering their effects on the world around. Therefore, here the activities create status changes for the greater world, which can be *positive*, *neutral* or *negative*. The activity of eating an ice-cream, for example, or watching an interesting movie may not generate any discernable amount of *positive* status changes for the world around, but still delivers pleasures to us. This type of hedonistic happiness can be further subdivided into two groups:

a) hedonistic type A, and

b) hedonistic type B

The activities in the pursuit of hedonistic type A happiness produce status changes that are *positive* for the *self,* and immaterial but *non-negative* for the world around. That is, they are not required to produce any status changes for the world around, but if they do, they are *positive.* For example, eating an ice cream produces status changes for the self in the form of positive sensation through taste; but the act produces practically no status changes for the world around. Participating in a group sports activity like playing soccer, for example, can be considered as another example of pursuit of hedonistic type A happiness, where the acts produce some *positive* status changes for the world around. In similar situations where the hedonistic activity creates *positive* status changes for the greater world around, the act can be considered eudaimonic also.

The hedonistic type B activities produce status changes, which are *positive* for the *self,* but *negative* for the world around. Here the overall status change tend to be *negative.* Sexual activities, for example, have the potential of producing tremendous amounts of hedonistic happiness; but depending on the circumstances, they can be either type A or type B. Inappropriate or non-consensual sexual behavior can provide hedonistic type B happiness for the self, while creating significant *negative* status changes for the victims. Business activities of corporations selling products which are harmful for the world while making monetary profits can also be considered as examples of hedonistic type B activities, because here some people benefit at the expense of greater world around. The activities of selling fossil fuels by the oil and gas industry without any effort to control the resulting global warming may be considered an example of hedonistic type B behavior, because here some folks are making money while contributing to the immensely *negative* status change of the climate change of the planet caused by the fossil fuel burning.

Thus, the activities creating the hedonistic type B status changes can produce overall *negative changes* in the world in the form of destructive acts, which can accumulate with time to reach crisis levels. Obviously, the activities creating this type *status changes* can be harmful for human evolution as it depends upon the creation of *positive changes*.

Thus, we can see a clear difference between the eudaimonic and the hedonistic types of happiness - specially between the eudaimonic and the hedonistic type B. Shifting peoples' fondness from hedonistic to eudaimonic happiness may sound wiser but not practical. A fulfilling life probably needs a balanced mix of both types of happiness, but the hedonistic type B happiness probably should be avoided as much as possible for the obvious reasons.

Pleasure - an encouragement for living

Pleasures are the secondary sources of happiness, which generally create very little or no *positive changes*. Sometimes they even create *negative changes*. We may ask, if activities are not creating *positive changes*, how do they generate the happiness! Let's explore the subject a bit. The elements of pleasure are like an inventory of benefits for just staying interested in life, because staying alive is the most important first step before we can take an active and meaningful role in promoting evolution by creating *positive changes* through our activities. The elements of pleasure are like membership benefits of a club, and their list grows larger in size as we evolve higher by expanding our activities. Most of the happiness from these secondary sources seem to be derived from the physical senses. Some basic examples are:

Eating tasty food for enjoyment
Listening to music
Enjoying a beautiful scenery

Having casual sex
Enjoying items of luxury
etc..

The simplest, and most important reward is, of course, the pleasure of eating food, but there are many other different sources of pleasure that can make us happy. In our societies, most of the time we can acquire these elements of pleasure with money without necessarily creating any noticeable *positive changes*. The capability to buy these elements of pleasures may increase our potential to create *positive changes* also, provided we have the proper mental setup to create them. Generally, it takes much less effort to find pleasures than to find happiness by creating *positive changes*. There are plenty of wealthy people, but probably only a minority of them use their wealth to create *positive changes*. Thus, the attitude seems to be the most important factor for the generation of *positive changes* in the world around.

Even though it seems easier to find happiness from pleasures than from activities that create *positive changes*, there are some serious drawbacks in finding our happiness from the elements of pleasure exclusively. The first one is that we may not have the ability to buy them all the time as we may be vulnerable to the ups and downs of our fortunes. The second negative point is that too much use of the elements of pleasure tends to reduce our sensitivity, causing a gradual decline of gratification out of them. If we start eating cakes every day instead of breads, we may not find the extra pleasure that we normally expect to get out of the cakes! Easy availability of the items of pleasure also tend to make people lazy and reluctant to pursue happiness through activities that could open new windows of the mind. The third negative point is that the some of the activities can generate *negative changes* for the greater world. Thus, it seems that it is okay to enjoy the elements of pleasure as long as they don't create *negative changes* in the world. Once we start using the elements that create *negative changes*, the greater world becomes vulnerable to miseries as explained in our theory of happiness. And, if the overall human culture starts creating overall *negative changes* consistently through peoples' activities, it will fall out of sync with the *force field of life*, meaning resisting evolution.

As we evolve higher, newer sources of pleasure are constantly being added to our menu. When man was living in the caves, his enjoyment from eating food was quite limited compared to today's eating pleasures out of numerous different culinary preparations. The early human also didn't have the books to read or the movies to watch in their list of things to enjoy. As we evolve by advancing our capabilities, we explore the world around us with the increased activities discovering newer elements of pleasure.

It seems that the basic three acts, eating, mating and protecting own territory can create primary as well as secondary sources of happiness - depending on the situation. For example, the *act of eating* makes us stay alive and thus the act creates large amounts of *positive changes*. But the act also opens up a world of eating enjoyment through the elaborate culinary preparations without creating any additional *positive changes* compared to the basic eating. To the contrary, some of the eating of fancy food for pleasure can be harmful to our health, and thus can create *negative changes*. Similarly, the act of mating creates *positive changes* by promoting our survival; but additionally, the act also opens up another world of pleasure through casual sexual activities for pleasure, without creating any appreciable *positive changes*.

The act of protecting the territory enables all others *positive acts* possible by eliminating the threats to the survival. The act also creates the necessary environment to feel protected and relaxed for getting engaged in other activities of life. In the absence of this protection, many activities of pleasure may not be possible. This *threat* to our *territory* can come in many different forms. Strangely, at present, in March of 2020, we are feeling one such threat, as the Coronavirus pandemic is happening in the USA and the world around. People in many parts of the country have been advised to stay at home, and most activities of pleasure have been severely restricted.

As the list of pleasures proliferate, people find their happiness with less effort from the large list of known sources rather than find new ones using their efforts - even if the quality of happiness may be inferior. Thus, people may gradually develop a lazy habit - the large number of easily available items of pleasure often become more attractive than the higher quality happiness to be found with efforts. Thus, finding happiness from the hedonistic[48,49] sources may be a natural trend of the affluent society.

There is another serious drawback of getting the majority of our happiness from the items of pleasure. Because the activities in their pursuit can sometimes produce overall *negative changes;* that is, they can cause *positive* status change for the *self,* but *negative* status changes for the greater world around! This way they deliver pleasure to a few while creating overall harm for the greater world. We see numerous examples of this happening on our planet on a regular basis. They vary from the next door neighbor's obsession with gambling activities ignoring his family's well being to the nation's powerful peoples' addiction to fossil fuel burning for monetary profits endangering our planet, when the profits are generally used to buy items of pleasure. In fact, perhaps most of the destructive activities of our planet are the results of the pursuit of hedonistic[48,49] type of happiness that have a net effect of harming the world. This may be the danger signal with this type of happiness. Probably, that's why human wisdom gave birth to spirituality that tend to downgrade the materialistic pleasures and recommend finding happiness from the higher sources having deep mental roots. Our *theory of positive changes* sees the justification in the philosophy.

Perhaps, that's why there is a natural consensus that the hedonistic sources of happiness are inferior to the eudaimonic ones. But it may not be realistic to build a complete and fulfilling practical life using only the eudaimonic type of happiness. There are just too many simple pleasures that make life so rewarding! But, the important guideline of our theory recommends to avoid creating the *negative changes*. Thus, it is okay to enjoy the pleasures of life, provided they do not produce *negative changes*. Fossil fuel burning is an example of an activity that creates *negative changes*. The use of fossil fuels have energized the industrial revolution that started in the late 18th century. It has produced many innovations and discoveries and created a huge amount of *positive changes*. Then, around the mid-twentieth century people learned that fossil fuel burning is causing serious harms to our planet by creating the global warming - thus creating overall *negative changes*. Therefore, soon after learning this fact we should have stopped the fossil fuel burning. But we have not been able to do that yet, and the act has become a destructive activity. There are many other destructive activities that resulted from the pursuit of pleasures causing overall *negative changes*. Pollution, overpopulation are good examples.

As We Evolve, Priorities Change

We are constantly evolving on many fronts, even though we also see significant amounts of destructive acts, which are accumulating and creating serious threats to our future survival. At every stage or level of evolution certain activities are more important than others for the survival; and thus they create the majority of *positive changes*, and deliver tremendous amounts of happiness. They can be considered as the primary acts for the creation of happiness. Then, as we evolve higher, challenges to our survival may change, and some newer and different activities become the primary acts, and start generating the majority of *positive changes.* Now the previous activities may not be needed as urgently for the survival as before, and may lose their degree of importance. These activities now may generate pleasures. They still generate *positive changes,* and can regain their primary status in a crisis situation.

For example, at the earlier states of evolution, eating, mating and protecting the territory were the most important activities for survival. Accordingly, those acts produced most of the *positive changes,* and certainly delivered tremendous amounts of happiness(pleasure). Then, gradually the advanced intelligence took over, and became more instrumental in helping the human species in their struggle for survival against the wild animals, who were much stronger physically. Thus, their various acts of intelligence created more *positive changes* than their acts of eating or mating, and thus created many new windows of happiness. Gradually, the acts of intelligence became progressively more important for their survival as the early man evolved to today's human. The acts of eating food and mating have remained essential activities for our survival, but at the current stage of evolution, our survival is not threatened because of lack of food or reproductive activities. Thus, those acts are now creating less amounts of *positive changes,* and, once the basic necessities are met, those acts can deliver pure pleasure without appreciable *positive changes.*

Thus it seems, as we evolve, our inventory of pleasures expands. The activities which were essential for our survival in the previous level of evolution are not as essential now, and accordingly they don't generate the same amounts of *positive changes* as before. They have become items of pleasure. Thus, pursuing predominantly the items of pleasure for our satisfaction through our activities may mean stagnating in the same level of evolution, and not trying to push its boundaries.

In summary, our theory says that we can maximize our chances of finding happiness if we develop an attitude of always trying to create *positive changes* with our activities whenever possible, and also enjoy the elements of pleasure, but select them in such ways that they do not create *negative changes*.

Other Shades of Happiness

Human mind has become progressively more advanced and complex with each climb to the next higher level of evolution. Consequently, the nature and the sources of happiness have also become progressively more complicated. For example, a form of happiness can be obtained from a relief or reduction of mental or physical stress. Stress can be equated with misery, and consequently, any reduction of stress is a *positive change*, and thus, it links with happiness. Sometimes an emotional relief also links with happiness. I remember a type of incident that happened to me few times in my life. It used to take place while I would be driving on the highway, when another car would cut in front of me rudely without signaling, when there was not enough space to do so. In this kind of situations, I would feel an emotional buildup inside me to do the same thing to him as a tit for tat even though it was not wise. And, I have to admit that I did this a few times, and felt happiness in the form of a satisfaction.

Most of these types of *happiness* are eccentric in nature, and do not help to build our stable foundation of happiness, probably because they do not satisfy the underlying science of happiness; i.e., they don't contribute in improving our survival, even in the most minute ways by creating true *positive changes*. Consequently, they may not be wise sources of happiness. But, the life is full of them! They generally have the potential of creating temporary and conditional *positive changes*, but have high amounts of uncertainties. My action in the example above was designed to make the other driver take notice, and change his driving style for the better in future - which is a conditional *positive change* with a low chance of happening.

Satisfying one's ego is probably another common way of finding a form of happiness. But often this act create more *negative* than *positive changes*. It does this by not recognizing the capabilities of others with an open mind, which can be a big hindrance in finding the right way in the different activity areas of life eventually leading to *negative changes*. Thus, the act often links with misery in the long run.

Religion and our Theory of Happiness

Religion and spirituality offer valuable guidance in our pursuit of happiness, but often we are not able to develop enough conviction in them consistently. Probably there are many reasons for this, but the main one may be that the advices of religion do not seek and use the support of logic and science. Another major reason may be that the interpretations of the religious messages often get distorted through preaching that get corrupted because of many factors. And, the situation gets worse when people are advised to use blind faith to follow those instructions. The system can influence large mass of people, and make them follow activities that can deviate from the true messages of religion. We have seen this happen time and again throughout the history of human civilization, which caused tremendous miseries to large number of people.

The theory of happiness, presented here, may be able to provide the needed scientific and logical support for the beneficial advises of religion, so that people can develop the needed conviction in them and follow them with sincerity. This can drastically reduce the amount of *negative changes* or destructive activities, and increase the possibilities of happiness by creating *positive changes* - and consequently, the possibilities of survival of the human race in the far future. Our *theory of positive changes* may sound a lot like a religion, and in fact, it does support the central concept of religion that everything in life is being controlled by a supreme force. It also says that we can maximize our chances of finding happiness if we always stay focused to create *positive changes* with our activities, while in our pursuit of happiness.

For example, let's take this basic age old wisdom, 'good deeds bring happiness'. This simple message is preached by religions, and other guidance sources, but often we don't take it seriously, most probably because no science or logic is provided. Our theory can provide the missing logical or scientific base to it. According to our theory, a 'good deed' is an activity which creates *positive changes* in the world around us. Thus, the activity stays in sync with the cosmic *force field of life* shrouding our planet, and links with happiness. 'Bad deeds', on the other hand, do the opposite, and link with misery. Therefore, the wisdom, 'good deeds bring happiness' is a logical truth, where a 'good deed' is defined as an act which creates *positive changes* in our world.

Thus, our theory of happiness makes a serious effort to unite science and religion on a common ground provided by the following truths:

a) a supreme force is exerting tremendous influence on all life on our planet; and

b) 'good deeds' invite happiness; while 'bad deeds' invite misery.

Additionally, the theory can provide us a simple check on the 'religious preaching' to see if the advice is truly beneficial or it is questionable. This can be determined by checking to see if it would produce a net *positive change* in the world around. This may be important, because, often we show the habit of following the herd, without checking what really we are following! This inquiry may act as a very important filter, that can enable us to detect the distorted interpretations of religious advices that may produce *negative changes* in our lives and in our world. This, unfortunately, we see happening quite often, throughout the history of human civilization!

Are we distorting our evolution!

Our instinctive *inner energy* is constantly urging us to align ourselves with the master cosmic *force field of life,* and we accomplish this by creating *positive changes* through our regular activities. The lower animals also perform the same routine, but because of the lack of advanced intelligence, they follow their instinct to stay in sync with this master force field. But, they respond more faithfully than the humans. Through their simple activities of life consisting mainly of eating, mating and protecting territory, they almost always create *positive changes*, and thus easily align themselves with the master *force field of life* to promote evolution. Our extra energy and the extra intelligence probably have given us some extra ammunition to go much further and take the evolution to higher levels faster; but it can also introduce distortion in our evolution, if we are not careful in planning our activities properly! It is like when we try to turn up the volume of a sound amplifier, distortion may creep in needing corrective action. Thus, our behavior can introduce distortions in our evolution as we try to accelerate it with our advanced intelligence. But, just like in the case of the sound amplifier, we think the distortion can be minimized and the evolution can be made more forceful by using proper guidelines.

Chapter Thirteen

The Nature of Human Evolution

An Afternoon at the Museum of Natural History:

One Saturday afternoon we were visiting the Smithsonian Museum of Natural History. There, in one area, it had displays describing the history of life on this planet. It showed how evolution has started with the simplest type of life forms, and has been picking up speed with today's most complex life form, the humans. It also showed that in the last few hundred years, this speed has been rising almost exponentially.

From the displays, a few astonishing facts stand out:

1) Life started 3.8 billion years ago, i.e., 3800000000 years ago, but the homosapien (man) appeared only about 200000 years ago.

Thus, the humans have been around for only about the last 0.005% of the time since life started. It's like if life started yesterday, the humans started to appear only about the last 5 seconds of yesterday! Truly amazing! A lot can happen in the future time left on this planet!

2) Serious and rapid human intellectual advancements started happening in only the last 200 years or so. Thus, it has started during the last 0.000005% of the time since life started. Using the previous analogy, if life started yesterday then serious human intellectual advancements started to happen only during the last 5 milliseconds, or 0.005 seconds of yesterday.

Thus, it feels like we have evolved from the cavemen to the users of high technology in just about the twinkling of an eye! So, it is logical to assume that there is almost unlimited potential of further innovation and growth in the future time of life on this planet. But in this short period of time, we also have stockpiled a tremendously high amount of destructive acts. They are accumulating and creating serious problems like the overpopulation, extreme pollution and the global warming, which are creating grave dangers for not only our future survival, but the mere existence of higher life on this planet!

Thus, in summary, on one hand we are creating tremendously high amounts of *positive changes,* and on the other hand we are generating very high amounts of *negative changes* through our activities. And both are happening at high rates. The *negative changes* are offsetting the *positive changes,* and are reducing the overall or net *positive changes* produced by our activities. Since the speed of our evolution depends upon the rate of production of the overall *positive changes* in our planet, the *negative changes* are reducing the effective speed of our evolution. And, since our survival depends on our evolution, when this speed is significantly slowed down, we may face many serious problems which can pose threats to our future survival.

To check whether or not the evolution is growing a disturbing trend of increasing *negative changes* resulting a distorted path with the humans or not, it may be helpful to compare the characteristics of our current evolution with those of the evolution at its earlier stages with the lower animals. It is logical to expect that at its earlier stages, evolution may be less vigorous but is happening in a purer form with less distortion. There we see that almost all the activities of the lower, simpler animals are focused towards promoting the central purpose of survival, creating *positive changes*. The activities of a fox, for example, consist primarily of eating, mating, and protecting its territory. All of these acts promote its survival. So, the fox generates almost all *positive changes*, and very little, if any, *negative changes* through its activities. And, this appears to be true for most lower animals. They are led by their instinct that works like a rigid railing of guidance, which they almost never step over with their limited intelligence. Thus, almost all the activities of the lower animals create *positive changes*. For them, the ratio of the *negative* to *positive* acts is almost zero or extremely low.

On the other hand, we the humans situated at the top of the evolutionary ladder, may not be able to boast a similar performance. With the help of our advanced intelligence, we have expanded our list of activities tremendously. They are extremely innovative and diverse. Like the lower animals, we also engage into the basic acts of eating, mating and protecting our territories, and create *positive changes* through them, and we also get involved in numerous other activities, many of which generate significant amounts of *positive changes*. But, unlike the lower animals, some of our activities produce significant amounts of *negative changes*. By doing so, we are opposing the most important requirement of evolution which is to create *positive changes* through our activities.

We use our advanced intelligence in making most of our decisions, most of the time overtaking our instinct. This gives us the capability to go much further and create much more *positive changes* than the lower animals as is reflected in the history, but it is also faltering at times and taking us in the wrong direction creating *negative changes*! And unfortunately, the human intelligence seems to be vulnerable to many distractions and temptations which often corrupt our judgment. Thus, it seems that we are using our advanced intelligence to produce high amounts of both, the *positive* and the *negative changes*. And, when compared with the lower animals at earlier stages of evolution, we are producing disproportionately higher amounts of *negative changes*. Consequently, the ratio of the *negative* to *positive acts* for us is much higher with us than with the lower animals. Thus, the trend line of our evolution seems to be getting steadily distorted signaling danger ahead for our future survival!

Science says, the universe is so vast that our planet is like a single grain of sand on the beach. Thus, logically, it is likely that there are other planets in the universe which have environments similar to ours, where similar *force fields* have been created by enormous cosmic energy bodies. The energies of those *force fields* probably have created life forms there, who have been going through a similar process of evolution to advance their capabilities. Also, perhaps there are some dead planets where life prospered once. Perhaps, there the life forms evolved with time, and found a new home somewhere else in the vast universe before the planet lost its life-sustaining qualities. Or perhaps, the life forms did follow a path of evolution, but couldn't evolve fast enough to develop the capabilities far enough to find another home elsewhere in the universe, and died with the planet!

Thus, it is quite possible that we may not have enough time here on this planet to evolve far enough by developing the required capabilities to survive in the universe beyond this planet by finding another home. But it is also possible that by developing enough capabilities our descendants may be able to find another home in the universe before our mother ship planet earth becomes unable to support life any longer. That's why a faster speed of evolution seems to be vitally important.

The *force field of life* is the controlling force; it defines the reference direction for the ideal track of evolution. Life forms try to adhere to this track by creating *positive changes* through their activities, which support the agenda of the force field. This is manifested by the nature of their activities through life, growth and evolution. Human activities create virtual personal force fields having components that are *in sync and/or out of sync* with the *force field of life*. The part that is in sync with the *force field of life*, creates *positive changes*, because it promotes similar activities of growth and prosperity like the *force field of life*. As explained before in our theory of happiness, the interaction of this component of *personal force field* with the surrounding *force field of life* is peaceful, which is responsible for the generation of the pleasant feeling called happiness. On the other hand, the part of our *personal force field* that is out of sync with the *force field of life*, generates *negative changes* in our world. They create a conflict or turbulence with the *force field of life*, and thereby increases the possibilities of unhappiness.

Thus, the *positive changes* created by our activities not only increase the speed of our evolution, but also our chances of finding happiness. Therefore, minimizing the *negative changes* is of paramount importance. But looking around, it seems that our accumulation of *negative changes* have gone up significantly giving rise to serious problems. And, it appears that the problems are getting more severe! But then, looking at the track record of human evolution we see that serious and rapid human intellectual advancements started happening in only the last 200 years or so. Thus, it has started during the last 0.000005% of the time since life started. Using the analogy used before, if life started yesterday then serious human intellectual advancements started to happen only during the last 5 milliseconds, or 0.005 seconds of yesterday. Therefore, anything is possible for the human race. We may need to make some course corrections by adjusting the nature of our activities, and use our efforts in the right direction. But, time is passing!

Exploring the sources of negative changes.

It seems that the majority of the serious *negative changes* are generated by unwise selection of activities that may reward the smaller inner circle, but do not benefit the greater world around. There are some notable contributors that cause this, such as *greed* or the *concept of profit*, etc., but the real cause may be our never-ending appetite for happiness, which is perfectly natural and is programmed by Nature to generate activities. The problem happens when we use shortcuts to find it, and then stay satisfied with a poorer version of it! This leads us to a convenient form of happiness, called *pleasure,* which is often found by low amounts of effort. The pursuit of *pleasures* often leads to the *hedonistic*[48,49] sources of happiness, which most often can be acquired without creating any appreciable amount of *positive changes* in the world around. To the contrary, often their pursuits lead to creation of significant amounts of *negative changes.* The flowchart of fig.1 shows how some of the problematic *negative changes* are being produced through our activities. It shows that the generation of the *positive* and/or the *negative changes* depends upon the type of happiness pursued.

Happiness is the ultimate prize of life. And, *greed* is a tremendously powerful urge. Thus, the *greed for happiness* can be a prolific driver of activities that generate both, the *positive* and the *negative changes.* The industrial revolution of the 18th and 19th centuries might have been started by necessities, but it probably was driven by the *greed* of a few who were not satisfied with what they possessed, and wanted more. This urge has produced numerous innovations and discoveries that have created a tremendous amount of *positive changes* by enriching the arts and the sciences of the human civilization.

But, by the same token, *greed* is also responsible, in one way or the other, for the creation of problems like the pollution, corruption, extreme inequality, etc. through the creation of overall *negative changes*. We have a habit of enjoying the fruits of the *positive changes* overlooking the harmful effects of the *negative changes* that accumulate with time adversely affecting the quality of our evolution. Thus, when we take a look at the history of human civilization, we see two faces of this strong drive called *greed*. The greed or the desire for happiness seem to be the creator of all activities of life.

Here is a flowchart of how some major *negative changes* are being introduced in our activities:

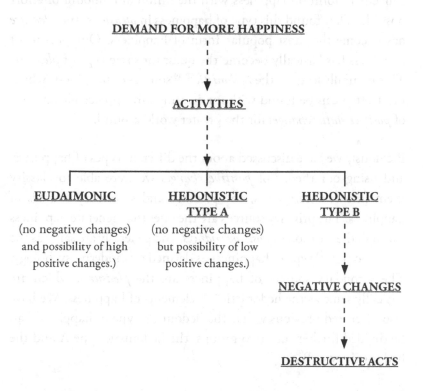

Fig.1

Multiple Happiness, multiple Choices

Most of the human activities generate a mix of *positive* and *negative* changes. In the *positive* acts, there are more *positive* than *negative* changes; while in the *negative* acts, there are more *negative* than *positive changes*. Most of the human activities in numerous different areas of life fall in one or the other of the above two categories. Furthermore, the majority of the acts are regular daily activities of life, while some are specialized acts generated by groups of people working under different organizations, large and small. There is one common tone behind most of these tremendous varieties of activities of life - it is that people are always trying to find a more convenient form of happiness with the minimum amount of effort possible. They found this type of happiness in *pleasures*, and *pleasure* has become the most popular form of happiness. Our pursuit of happiness has basically become the quest for some type of *pleasure*. This naturally leads to the *hedonistic*[48,49] sources of happiness, which most often can be found without creating any appreciable amount of *positive status changes* for the greater world around.

Previously we have discussed about the different types of happiness, and using our theory of *positive changes* we were able to classify them into two categories, the primary and secondary sources of happiness. The primary sources are the ones that generate happiness through the creation of *positive changes*, and generally are same as the eudaimonic[48,49] type of happiness as defined by modern psychology. The secondary sources of happiness are the *pleasures*, which are basically same as the hedonistic[48,49] elements of happiness. We have also discussed previously that the hedonistic type of happiness can be divided further into two groups, the hedonistic type A and the hedonistic type B.

The hedonistic type A activities are designed to generate happiness primarily for the self by creating *positive status changes* for the smaller inner circle. But, they can also create *positive status changes* for the world around, which can vary from being negligible to truly significant. One of the main features of the hedonistic type A activities is that they do not create *negative changes*. That is, the activities do not have any harmful effects for the greater world. Thus, in summary, a hedonistic type A activity produces a *positive status change* for the self, and no *negative status change* for the greater world around; it may or may not produce any *positive status changes* for the world around. Numerous regular activities of life fall in this category, e.g. eating an ice cream or listening to a favorite music, etc..

In the case of the hedonistic type B happiness, the activities provide happiness for the self, but they also create harmful effects in the world around. Here the act of pursuing the happiness produces a *positive status change* for the self only and perhaps for the inner circle, but *negative status changes* for the greater world around. Thus, overall it is a *negative change*. This means that the activities looking for hedonistic type B happiness have the potential of becoming destructive acts. Looking around in the world we can see many examples of this type of activities, small and large. Some of them are generating significant amounts of *negative changes,* which are accumulating and creating problems like the extreme pollution, the climate change, and so on, a are posing serious threats to the future survival of the human species. Although the hedonistic Type A activities seem to be benign pleasure-seeking acts, they have a natural tendency to cross over from the type A to the type B, unless precautions are taken.

Thus, it seems that the popularity of the hedonistic type of happiness may be a major cause for the production of the high amounts of *negative changes* in today's world. There probably are many reasons for this popularity of the hedonistic happiness, but one of the main reasons may be that this type of happiness can be found more easily, with less effort and without the serious participation of the physical and mental capabilities of a person. Also, most of the times, it can be bought with money and enjoyed at a convenient time and place, and the pleasure can be turned on quickly.

By comparison, it is more difficult to extract happiness from the eudaimonic type of sources. Part of this difficulty lies in the fact that the pursuit of those sources of happiness often require the participation of the mind to be successful. Moreover, most of the times they also require some effort. Furthermore, the eudaimonic sources of happiness start to develop slowly in seemingly subtle and mild ways - not as intense and quick as the hedonistic types. But like the ocean, they generally start shallow but gradually leads to enormous depth - much higher than with the hedonistic sources.

The Money System:

In Nature, life revolves around a system of activities and rewards. The right acts that promote Nature's agenda are rewarded with happiness of in some form. The lure of the rewards make life forms get engaged in activities in the their pursuit. These rewards come in the form of a pleasant feeling of happiness of some type, which are acquired by activities that promote Nature's agenda, which is promoting the project of evolution of life. This is achieved by promoting the survival of species, which, in turn, achieved by activities that create *positive changes.* For example, the basic activities of eating, mating or protecting their territories support the survival of life forms; and thus they create *positive changes;* and consequently those activities deliver happiness(pleasure) to the creatures. They repeat those activities to get more pleasures, and thus the routine of activities of life are generated, which in turn, build the process of evolution. The lure of the *reward* urges life forms to stretch their capabilities through progressively more difficult challenges. Thus, a happiness in some form is the *reward,* which is the driver of Nature's system of activities that promotes its project of evolution of life on this planet.

Perhaps, in an effort to copy the Nature's system of activities and rewards, and at the same time to make it more controllable and organized, man has devised his own system of activities and rewards. It works similarly to the Nature's system, but it uses money as its central reward. The system is meant to give out rewards of money to the deserving people who are contributing towards the growth and prosperity of the society with their activities. Those acts in the long run are expected to create an effect to promote the human survival and prosperity, and in turn, human evolution by creating *positive changes* as in the Nature's system. Thus, instead of getting rewarded directly with *happiness* in some way as in the Nature's system, the deserving person gets an award of monetary benefits. It is assumed that the money, in turn, is going to provide the person the capability to buy elements of happiness of choice, at the person's own convenient time and place.

The money system tries to convert the rewards in measurable units, and has its own merits and flaws. Here, the amount of reward can be controlled by simply adjusting the amount of money given as rewards. Being a form of wealth, the monetary reward has a direct and realistic appeal. Also with the money a person can to buy *happiness* at a future time. But, the system has some serious flaws also. First of all, the system needs to be able to perform a fair and precise evaluation of the accomplishment of the person by considering:

a) whether the action of the person created true *positive changes,* i.e. whether the act really benefited the greater world(human species); and also

b) how beneficial was the accomplishment for the greater
world, i.e.,how large or deep is the *positive change* generated
by the action of the person!

Those information are needed to grant the proper amount of
monetary reward, which is supposed to be proportional to the
amount of the *positive changes* created by the action of the person.
Obviously these are not easy tasks. It is difficult to make a correct
evaluation of the activity's contribution towards the generation of
positive changes created since it is subjective, and can't be measured
in units. Many flaws of the human character like bias, nepotism and
politics can come into play corrupting the system. Thus, gradually,
the true meaning of a *positive* act can get lost, and the system may
lose its effectiveness. Often, people may get rewarded for activities
that generated little or no *positive changes*. Also, often the wrong
people may get rewarded, while the deserving people may be left out
in our monetary reward system.

Also, beyond the basic needs, the monetary rewards tend to
encourage people to buy elements of pleasure which generate low
amounts of *positive changes*. Thus, our monetary reward system
keeps on giving out money as rewards, and people stay satisfied with
the *pleasures* bought with the money. The system seems to encourage
people to get engaged in mostly hedonistic type of happiness -
without really urging them to make the effort to create true *positive
changes*. Gradually, this has become the general trend of the human
civilization, which probably is one of the main reasons why our
evolution is getting distorted and stagnant with low amounts of
positive changes being created through our activities.

To rectify this flaw of the monetary reward system, the activities
deserving rewards must link somehow, directly or indirectly, with
the ultimate purpose, which is the promoting of the survival of the
human species. This means that there should be a requirement that

the activities deserving rewards have to create *positive changes*. When we insert this requirement into our monetary rewards system, the problem in the existing system becomes obvious. Many acts, for which people get rewarded in our existing system, seem to generate little or no *positive changes; i.e.*, they don't seem to promote the survival of the human species at all! To the contrary, they often generate *negative changes* by adversely affecting our survival chances as a species! The profit making activities of the oil and gas industries, for example, are doing serious damage to the life-supporting environment of this planet by encouraging fossil fuel burning. Many corporations manufacturing chemical products that produce short term benefits through increased convenience but long term harms also fall in this group. There are many other examples of human activities getting rewarded in our monetary reward system that are actually doing harm to the future survival of the human race!

There is also another significant issue which is cultural in nature. In a system where the amount of wealth decides the degree of success of the person, people try to become wealthy through devious ways sacrificing things of high values of life, thus creating serious *negative changes*. The money system may be encouraging a materialistic culture which tends to downplay the development of mental qualities, which seems to go against the overall trend of higher evolution.

The Concept of Profit

The financial framework of the world is supported by the monetary profits earned by corporations. It is then distributed to their workers, who then earn their livings through the wages and salaries, etc.. Thus, *profit* plays a huge role in human society. It also has enormous influence on the attitude and behavior of people in the society. We tend to translate all types of gains in terms of monetary profits, even though this kind of thinking seems to have a serious flaw. Since the *profit* is the main driver of most of human activities in the practical world, a *profit* making activity should create *positive changes* in the world around. But in reality, many of our important projects fail to do so. In fact, many of them actually create *negative changes* in the world by adversely affecting the future survival of the human race. But they seem to be able to get the approval of our societies because of this flaw in our concept of *profit*.

In another example, if we take a look at the crimes committed by people every day, we may see that this same distorted concept of profit is again the reason behind many of them. And, this distortion may be affecting the nature of our evolution adversely by influencing the people to act ways that produce *negative changes*. Some pockets of wisdom may be available from spirituality, but they are not reaching the street probably because people have not been able to develop enough conviction in them. So, we seem to be carrying this cultural flaw through generations like kicking the can down the road.

Entrepreneurs of the society are on the constant hunt for monetary profits. Quite frequently they seem to have the talents and tools to lead the drive for the human race to evolve higher, but their efforts are getting short-circuited by the flawed concept of *profit*. Consequently, the human civilization is not generating as much *positive changes* as it could, and this may be reflected in the distortion of our evolution.

There are also some systemic secondary factors that contribute to the creation of the *negative changes*. Examples include *destructive competitiveness, wealth inequality,* etc.. Thus, it appears that *negative changes* are being produced by many standard elements of our society. They may be stealthily distorting the nature of our evolution even without us realizing it! Thus, as we evolve higher, a lot of our increased capabilities are getting wasted in producing *negative changes*.

The situation reminds me of an experiment that I was performing many years ago in our college lab while studying Electronics. I was working on a project to design and build a radio amplifier. A radio amplifier, by the way, is an electronic device that picks up very faint radio signals from the air, and then processes and amplifies them many times when we can hear them loud and clear. The design was completed and amplifier was built. Then it was time to test its performance. It was found that the sound coming out was loud enough, but it was distorted - specially when the volume was turned up! The reason for the distortion was that the incoming radio signal was mixed with noise, and the device was amplifying both, so that the sound at the output was distorted because of the presence of the noise.

The solution was quite simple and straight forward. I had to find a way to prevent the noise signals from getting amplified along with the desired radio signals. Incorporating a filter at the input that selectively blocked out most of the unwanted noise signals but allowed the desired radio signals to pass through, did the job nicely. The distortion was minimized, and the sound coming out was loud and clear, even when the volume was raised.

Chapter Fourteen

Decoding an Ancient Wisdom

<u>The Advaita Vedanta, Science, Evolution</u>
<u>and the theory of *Positive Changes:*</u>

People may or may not be spiritual, but spirituality is an important element of life, because it influences many of the vital trends of the human civilization. Science, obviously, is important too, because it helps us in real life to survive and enjoy life by advancing our capabilities. People most commonly link with spirituality through their religions or philosophies that act like religion. Thus, it would be extremely beneficial for the human race if science and religion could work together to go forward by planning a progressively better future for the humans, and perhaps for all life on this planet.

While most religions and philosophies may have many great features, some accept or support science better than others. One particular criterion may be a good determining factor! It is the acceptance of the theory of evolution, the very important scientific theory that uncovers the history of life on this planet. It was discovered by Charles Darwin in the mid 19th century. The Advaita Vedanta, originated in the 8th century CE by Adi Shankaracharya, with its roots going back to the oldest Upanishads accepts the theory of evolution most naturally and effortlessly. In fact, the theory of evolution seems like its natural extension.

The entire Advaita Vedanta can be summarized in one important verse, which says:

Brahma satyam jagat mithya, jivo brahmaiva naparah

In a nutshell, it means, the Brahma(Brahman) is the only truth, the world is an illusion, and there is ultimately no difference between Brahman and the individual self of a person(Atman). This wisdom can be divided into three parts:

The Brahma(Brahman) is the only truth,
the world is an illusion, and
there is ultimately no difference between Brahman and the Atman.

The first part of the verse talks about the source of our origin, and our oneness. A supreme cosmic energy, mostly created by Sun is the creator of all life on this planet. We ourselves are made of fragments of this energy enclosed inside our unique material bodies. Thus, we truly have the same identity, being products of the same source, and are its subjects. The Vedanta basically says this truth. The Brahman of the Vedanta points towards the force field of life created by Sun.

The second part of the verse is truly intriguing. It says that all the activities of life are actually 'maya's or illusions! The Vedanta is implying here that all the worldly affairs are just temporary realities - there is an absolute reality or purpose behind the worldly affairs. To find out what this purpose is, we need to analyze deeply the activities of life. And, to accomplish this, we need to use Charles Darwin's theory of evolution, which was conceived much later in the 19th century CE. Human activities are too complex to start with, so to have a clear understanding of the mechanism of the 'maya's, let's begin with the activities of the lower animals. Human acts follow the same mechanism.

Most of the activities of the fox, for example, can be divided into three basic categories, eating, mating and protecting its territory. The first two are the primary acts, and the third one makes the first two possible. The animal is driven to these activities by the lure of a reward, which is the pleasure of the activity. The animal gets hooked on to this reward and keeps on coming back to repeat these acts. The cycle is repeated for generations until an important event takes place! A minute physical mutation happens to the animal, which enhances its survival capabilities. With the improved capabilities, the new fox gains survival advantages over others by natural selection as explained by Darwin's theory, and rises to a higher level of evolution. The animal then creates new generations of foxes with similar enhanced capabilities through reproduction, who keep on repeating the same or perhaps slightly more expanded list of activities, and wait for the next positive physical change to happen that will help them evolve to the next higher level of evolution. This perpetual cycle of life keeps on running on all forms of life including the humans, promoting higher evolution of life on this planet. Thus, just as the Vedanta says, all the activities of life seem to be temporary realities or 'maya's to serve the higher purpose of evolution of life on this planet.

One important requirement of higher evolution should be noted here. The positive physical mutation is activated or utilized only by appropriate activities. Lower animals accomplish this easily, because their changes are simple and obvious - the appropriate activities to utilize them are found almost automatically. But for the humans these changes are happening in the areas of intelligence, which are often challenging to detect. Thus, it is possible that the plumber who came to fix our faucet was a potential Math prodigy, who didn't follow the appropriate line of activities to take advantage of his latent genius.

Evolution is built of numerous minute *positive change*s happening to the life forms. Thus, the element of *positive change* is the building block of evolution. This way life forms have evolved from the simple single cell organisms to today's human. And it may not be the endpoint of evolution on this planet. Perhaps, the humans can keep on evolving higher by developing newer capabilities, and survive beyond this planet to become a living entity of this universe! Thus, survival is the most important criterion of life, and evolution is the most important event happening to life forms on this planet. Therefore, the purpose behind the 'maya's is the most important one for all life on this planet. In the 8th century CE, the facts about evolution were not known, and so the Vedanta closed the chapter after correctly pointing at the presence of the bigger purpose behind the worldly affairs - without identifying what this purpose actually is. The chapter was reopened a thousand years later in the mid 19th century with the discovery of the science of evolution of life by Charles Darwin. Thus, the concept that was originated by the Advaita Vedanta was completed a thousand years later by the theory of Evolution.

The third part of the verse says that we are same as the Brahman. That is, we are created by the Brahman(the cosmic force field of life), and have the same latent qualities. We should realize this, and implement these qualities in promoting the plan of the Brahman, which is to carry out higher evolution of life. As mentioned before, the element of *positive change* is the building block of evolution. Thus, creating *positive change*s through our mental and physical activities is the way to promote evolution. The Vedanta also says that once this realization comes, and we and act accordingly, we move forward towards enlightenment or the state of unlimited happiness. Thus, creation of *positive change*s links with happiness. The completed concept provide the following wisdom:

1) We all are brothers and sisters, created from the same supreme cosmic source, and are here to serve an important purpose together.

2) All the activities of life are actually temporary realities serving the central purpose of promoting higher evolution of life on this planet through creation of *positive changes*.

3) Enlightenment or the state of unlimited happiness happens when we realize that we have latent Brahman-like virtues; and apply them to create *positive changes* in the world around promoting higher evolution. This implies that happiness is found through activities that have the potential of promoting higher evolution through the creation of *positive changes*.

Perhaps, this new concept should be called the Naba Vedanta or New Vedanta, as it incorporates science and logic in its wisdom. The concept is saying that the Nature's directive to all life forms is to select and use the appropriate activities to utilize the potentially beneficial minute biological changes that have been happening to them mostly randomly over long periods of time, and thus promote the survival of their species promoting evolution. For the lower animals on the evolutionary ladder, it has been easier to select the appropriate activities that promoted their evolution from their routine of activities because the factors that promoted their survival were simpler and mostly physical in nature. But now, for the humans at the top of the evolutionary ladder, the factors that promote their evolution are intellectual in nature, and thus it is infinitely more difficult to determine and utilize the routine of activities that would boost their evolution.

This concept says that the right acts promote evolution by supporting the survival of the species, and are rewarded with happiness in some form. Science says that the survival of a species is promoted by *positive change*s occurring in the status of the species through the random natural biological changes, which are utilized by appropriate activities of the life form, and converted to *positive change*s. Thus, it can be said:

beneficial biological change x appropriate activity => Evolution

The idea of this concept can be used to check to see if the humans are using the right activities to promote evolution! First of all, the behavior of the lower animals can be analyzed to have a base of comparison. There, at the lower levels of evolution, the process seems much weaker but perhaps purer, because the advanced intelligence has not developed yet to interfere with the natural instinct, which seems to be a product of the influence of the *force field of life*. These animals have a simple and basic routine of activities, consisting mostly of eating, mating and protecting their territories. When these acts are analyzed, it is found that all of them promote the survival of the species and deliver happiness(pleasures) to them. And then, when a minute potentially beneficial physical change happens, their basic list of physical activities is generally adequate to utilize the change to advance their survival capabilities, which are also mostly physical in nature. Thus, the lower animals are satisfying the hybrid concept, and are obeying the directive of Nature quite faithfully.

We, the humans, on the other hand are sitting on the highest perch of the evolutionary ladder, and are using advanced intelligence to plan most of our important activities. Our potentially beneficial biological changes are probably happening in the area of intelligence, which are difficult to detect and then utilize with the right activities. Our capabilities to promote evolution have increased immensely, but so have our destructive activities, which have increased significantly creating severe problems to our well being and to our survival in the far future. Looking at the accomplishments of the human race, we see numerous acts of tremendous innovations, but many of those innovations have not improved our chances of survival as a human species as much as they have created threats to our survival in the future! It seems that they are focused to earn more money and more pleasure rather than to create *positive changes!*

Therefore, the concept is advising the humans to get involved in progressively more challenging and complex activities to make sure they can utilize the potentially beneficial biological change that may be happening inside their areas of intellect. And, the key requirement of all those acts would be that they all shall create *positive changes.* Thus, instead of discouraging people from getting involved in the worldly affairs for the fear of getting corrupted, this hybrid concept encourages people to get engaged in activities - but in the right ways, using appropriate activities that promote the survival of the human species. The concept also gets the support of the Upanishads as they say that enlightenment can be reached through different paths of activities that create *positive changes.* It seems that this concept can have profound implications on human cultures by advising people to get engaged in activities that create *positive changes.* Of course, it will be fine to include some acts that provide pure pleasure with little or no *positive changes* like eating an ice cream or listening to our favorite music, for example. But the concept advises people to refrain from activities that create *negative changes* by causing an overall harm to our species.

Chapter Fifteen

Some Case Studies

Here we are going to see how some of our everyday regular behaviors and activities play out in the environment of the *force field of life!* They may be known to us as obvious producers of happiness or misery, but here let's see if they support our theory showing that the acts that generate *positive changes* link with happiness and the acts that generate *negative changes* associate with misery!

(1) Pleasure of eating food

The first and foremost act of promoting evolution is, of course, eating; because In order to promote evolution, a life form has to stay alive first. And, then it has to get involved in other activities to play a meaningful role in the activities of life. Thus, the act of 'eating' generates the most important *positive changes,* and the reward is the pleasure of eating, which is probably the strongest attraction of life.

(2) Love, the ultimate medium

When we hear the word *Love,* a huge territory of perception is covered, and our instinct says that the *force field of life* somehow has a direct link with this element of life. Perhaps, like the magnetic force creating the medium of the magnetic force field, the *force field of life* is creating the medium of *love,* which makes birth, growth and evolution of life possible.

We see many different types of relationships based on *love.* Of course, the most popular and well known is the romantic love, when, typically, a male and a female are attracted towards each other. Mother Nature assumes that this love affair is a prelude to the extremely important act of reproduction, which promotes the process of evolution, creating *positive changes.* And so, she attaches a large amount of reward in the form of pleasure or happiness. This *love* is mostly sexual in nature but depending on the nature and attitude of the participants, it can transform into other types of *love,* and keep on creating further *positive changes.*

Then there is *love* in the form of affection or nurture - between the parents and their children, between the grand-parents and their grandchildren, between siblings and between close relatives. It can also exist in many other relationships, such as that between the teachers and their students, between the preachers and their followers, and so on. Like a climbing pole to a young plant, nurture helps the recipients grow properly by providing the right guidance, and thus it creates *positive changes* bringing happiness to the nurture provider.

The most basic and powerful example of love probably lies in the relationship between a mother and her child. The mother spends a lot of her resources nurturing the child. In return, she finds a profound form of mental happiness for the *positive changes* she creates through the growth of the child. Both parents of the child get rewarded with tremendous enjoyment they get in nurturing the child. Here, excessive use of toys may change the chemistry of the situation, and adversely affect the *positive changes* created by the activity by interfering with the natural development of human bond, and the mental development of the child. To a child, a lonely room fitted with toys may not seem like a gift, but more like a punishment of a solitary confinement - specially at night, when the baby wants the warmth of his/her mother.

We also see instances, when two good friends are very *fond* of each other. They help each other when needed, and one stands by the other when one of them faces a difficult time. Thus, they join their resources, and get more things done than each of them could accomplish themselves individually. Here, *love* happens through the form of friendship, which can create *positive changes* in their worlds bringing happiness.

Probably, we all have noticed that while learning a subject, or working on a project, or doing something, we perform better when we develop a liking for it. Something happens, and things fall in sync to create *positive changes*. This 'liking' is also a kind of *love*.

(3) Happiness/pleasure from Sex

The reproductive activity or "having sex" is probably the second most important act of promoting evolution. The act creates fresh new lives to replace the old and weary ones to carry on the activities of life with more vigor, creating the possibility of generation of greater amounts of *positive changes*. Thus, the act helps us stay in sync with the *force field of life* rewarding us with pleasure and happiness.

Since the act is immensely important for sustaining the process of evolution, Nature or the cosmic *force field of life* has attached a huge amount of reward to this activity for the participating partners. For the lower life forms, it probably comes mostly through simple physical pleasures, but for humans this reward comes through both, the physical and mental pleasures and happiness.

The most important *positive change* created by this activity is the promise of the birth of a new life to carry on the process of evolution with fresh vigor, and the initial reward may be limited to mostly the physical pleasure. The participants receive this reward even when they may be fooling Mother Nature by actually not having babies by artificially preventing pregnancy, but she assumes that the offspring is on the way. Thus we derive pleasures from casual sex and other similar sexual acts. For the humans, the sexual intimacy can also bring the participants mentally closer, and they can harmonize and unite their individual mental energies to create larger *positive changes* in many different areas of life, creating happiness in those areas.

By the same token, for partners without a mental sync, sexual activities may have the possibilities of creating very limited *positive changes,* and may offer only the happiness through physical pleasure. They may not open too many new windows of happiness. The only *positive change* in this situation seems to be the possibility of the birth of new lives. Thus the possibility of happiness in this kind of relationship may be limited. The solution may be to explore the possibilities of creating *positive changes* through other activities as well.

Also, there is the possibility of a significant drawback in depending too much on this natural, but easy source of happiness from sexual activities. Its super strong urge can inhibit and overtake all other drives, and thus cause our intellectual growth to be stunted. The result may be that less amounts of *positive changes* generated from other activities, which in turn, may create limited happiness.

The importance of sexual acts and their link with the reward of happiness is exhibited more clearly with the lower animals. Male animals fight violently to earn the right to have sex with the female of their choice, often at the risk of serious injury, or even death. The females seem to show a clear preference for males with superior physical vigor, who can have a competitive edge in procuring food, finding mates and protecting their territories. This behavior, again, promotes the process of evolution, by creating *positive changes* through their offspring.

In humans, with the advancement of intelligence, a couple of intellectual elements have been added to the list of basic physical attributes to decide the superiority of the males - the mind and the intelligence. In fact, they tend to outweigh all other physical characteristics in the contest of superiority. They also play dominant roles in finding maximum pleasure from human sexual behaviors - the mental intimacy play a big part in enhancing the pleasure(happiness) of physical intimacy. In fact, it has effects which probably go well beyond the physical boundaries of the sexuality. Perhaps, it can uplift our existence and promote evolution, not just through physical perpetuation, but also in other nonphysical ways.

But having sex is like signing a two-part contract with Mother Nature, for promoting evolution! The first part is the reproductive activity, and enjoying the reward from Mother Nature, in the form of intense pleasure. The second part lies in supporting and nurturing the offspring to a stage, where the child can play his/her own role in the process of evolution. So, many possibilities of *positive* and/or *negative changes,* and consequently of happiness or misery exist in this area, which depend on corresponding activities.

c) Riding the tightrope of affairs:

The human animal may not be naturally monogamous. Mother nature may want us to get as many different combinations as possible, to increase the likelihood of the birth of a superior being, who may be able to advance the evolution more significantly than the average. So, it is possible that Mother Nature might have created a natural urge in us to meet and mate with different individuals! But it may be the crude natural truth; we have come a long way since then.

Happiness depends on the overall *status change.* If it is *positive,* possibilities of happiness increase; if it is *negative,* possibilities of misery increase. Here the variables in the equation are the response of the partners and people having close relation with them. Children, if any, may have the biggest contribution to the *status change,* because they are prime players for promoting the process of evolution, and have the potential of creating huge amounts of *positive* or *negative changes.*

e) Inappropriate sexual behavior:

Inappropriate sexual behaviors link with sex but still generally produce unhappiness in the long run! The reason is that those behaviors create other variables in the equation in addition to sex. They generate *negative changes,* so that the overall *status change* becomes *negative* in these situations. Generally, these variables are the harms done to the victims who typically are the children and the young folks of the society.

f) Sex in senior years of life:

There is probably nothing wrong in getting enjoyment out of sex in the senior years of life, but it is like opening a spring window in the fall. This is a window on the garden side which is used to watch all the young plants grow. Sex opens a large window of pleasure, most of which are created through birth and nurture of new lives. It also opens other related windows next to it, which are normally associated with youth, growth, and extravagant spending of energy, a large part of which is used in trials and errors in the pursuits of happiness of many different types. Here the feelings of the success and failures of which can be profound and intense.

Thus, it seems that sexual activities in the senior years are not meant to produce much lasting happiness, because it doesn't produce much *positive changes* through the birth of an offspring. But not all is lost there, because *positive changes* can be created through different types of activities, which can bring different kinds of happiness. Many of these activities are planned around helping others, i.e., creating *positive changes* in the lives of others. And since a true *positive change* is defined as a *positive status change* for the entire human race, all *good* deeds are counted towards the happiness of the human soul. So, we can open the window on the other side, where we can see the mountains, the river, and the valley - the serenity, wisdom and freedom of the mind, and all the other mental stuff; but an occasional trip on the garden side would be just fine!

---

(4) Money:

Money we can buy the basic needs and the protection for our lives, e.g., by buying better food, better healthcare, and many other direct, and indirect protections. Thus, it can create *positive changes* and link with happiness.

We have a perennial question in our mind, whether an extra amount of wealth beyond the basic needs can increase the amount of happiness proportionately higher! Recent researches[50] show that this is not the case. It is found that happiness seems to increase with wealth, but only up to a certain point which is beyond but not too far from the point where the basic needs are met. Beyond that area the track of happiness appears to flatten up, or even can decrease. Our theory of *positive changes* supports these findings. Happiness depends upon the creation of *positive changes*. In the basic needs zone, the creation of *positive changes* depend almost directly upon the wealth; but beyond that zone the extra wealth does not necessarily produce a proportional amount of *positive changes*. It now depends more on the state of our mind and our attitude.

With the extra money, people tend to buy more of elements of pleasure, where *pleasure* is a different type of happiness. It is predominantly hedonistic, and does not generate much *positive changes*. It is not as profound as a true happiness, which is mostly eudaimonic in nature. Also, there are a few problems in relying too much on *pleasure* as our rewards of life. The first one is that we may not have the ability to buy them all the time because we are vulnerable to the ups and downs of our fortunes. The second one is that, excessive dependence on them can gradually reduce our sensitivity towards them. As a result, we may need progressively more elements of pleasure to get the same amount of satisfaction. Thus, it may not be possible to increase our happiness by increasing our elements of pleasure. c it appears that money can provide us happiness up to a certain point, which is not much higher than the point where the basic needs are met. Beyond this point the quality of happiness seems to degrade because of the lack of generation of significant amount of *positive changes,* and people start getting the version of *happiness* called *pleasure.* This, of course, can change if the person uses his wealth to create activities that generate *positive changes,* for example helping others and so on.

By the way, the money system of the human civilization has influenced, and perhaps changed Nature's system of *activity and rewards* that promotes the process of evolution. In Nature's system, life forms are encouraged with the lure of a reward to get engaged in activities, some of which create minute *positive changes*, which sustains the process of evolution. The *reward* is a happiness of some form; including *pleasures*. The superior ape probably learned and applied a new trick to get the pleasure of eating a new source of food, which others didn't, and thus created a *positive change* for its species and promoted its evolution.

Man has copied this *activity-reward* system of Nature, and designated money as the reward for the deserving people. The system assumes that the money can be used to buy happiness. Here the first problem is that sometimes some of these so-called *deserving people* are creating very little *positive changes* - to the contrary, many are being paid for activities that are creating *negative changes!* There lies one seed of unhappiness in our monetary reward system!

Secondly, these monetary rewards are not being used to encourage generation of more *positive changes*. While some of these rewards do create *positive changes* by providing the important basic needs, a large part is generally used to buy elements of *pleasure,* a form of happiness that do not necessarily create *positive changes.* As a result, our monetary reward system is not very efficient in encouraging production of *positive changes* through our activities! This may be introducing a distortion in the quality of our evolution. This distortion is piling up destructive activities, which are creating serious obstacles on our path forward! There lies another seed of unhappiness!

137

(5) Happiness from Marriage

The human animal may not be created to be monogamous by Nature!
In order to avoid unnecessary fighting and feuds, our society has invented the system of marriage, so that the opposite sexes can unite and enjoy their lives in a disciplined way. Then, they can join their unique strengths to create *positive changes* in many directions, and open many windows of life through which happiness can come in to their lives.

First of all, the reproductive activities promote the process of evolution, and so they bring a lot of happiness to the partners.

I remember one my close friend's sister was very timid when she was single. She mostly stayed with her books and music. But then she married a man who loved the outdoors. Now she has rediscovered herself.

Different phases of the married life promote the process of evolution differently. Consequently, happiness comes with different intensities at different times of the marriage. In the beginning, most of the promoting of evolution is done through giving births to new individuals - the children. So, most of the happiness comes from reproductive activities. The element of romance can start to dissipate slightly.

In the next phase, proper rearing of the children with love, nurture and guidance is very important for the process of evolution. Then they can grow with exuberance, and mature as strong human specimens, and start promoting evolution themselves more effectively. So, a large reward of happiness is attached by Mother Nature to bringing up of children in the life of the married person. The element of romance can dissipate further at this stage of marriage.

Further down the road of the married life, the element of romance between the two can totally disappear. It may be a large negative change, but probably totally natural, because romance was a prelude to dating. At this mid-life stage, the material and mental resources of two individuals can unite to create large *positive changes* around them. Other elements like loyalty, and friendship can create a bond, and become more important in creating more *positive changes*. The growing children also strengthen the bond, and can create even more *positive changes* in the family. The net change can be positive to give them *happiness.*

Whether there will be *happiness* or *misery* in the family may be decided whether the net change is *positive* or *negative.* It will depend upon the mental chemistry of the couple, which will, in turn, depend upon how ardently they are striving to create positive changes in their worlds.

(6) Happiness from children

Children are the most vital carriers of Nature's process of evolution because they have the highest potential to accelerate the process. Each child has the potential to create a tremendous amount of *positive changes*, and also has the latent potential to be a superior specimen. So, nurturing, and taking care of children are *positive* acts to promote the process of evolution, and thus are rewarded with happiness in many different ways. It is a very common and well known fact that parents wish that their children become 'better' than they are. This is also an urge to promote evolution and to stay in sync with the *force field of life.* Activities supporting this *wish* link with happiness.

Actually, activities helping children grow open quite a few windows of happiness. Parents put up a tremendous efforts bringing up children, and often make great sacrifices in the way. Nurturing love tends to flow from the older to the younger generation. This is because the younger ones need the protection to grow, and also they have more possibilities to contribute to the evolutionary process.

Divorces are common occurrences among families, more in some countries than others. They bring large *negative changes* to the lives of the children, and also their parents, which often become the major causes of unhappiness. Thus, in summary, having a positive connection with children is one of the most effective way of linking with happiness.

(7) Rating the different types of happiness

Happiness in its many different forms and shades seems to be the lure and driver all activities of life. Human activities in the pursuit of happiness can produce different types of *status changes* in our personal world and in the world around. A person's activities that produce *positive or* beneficial *status changes* for the self, seem to deliver happiness to the person. These acts may also produce *positive status changes* for the greater world around, but they may also be neutral or even *negative* for world around. Thus, our acts in the pursuit of happiness can be divided into two main types:

1) Efforts that try to create overall positive status changes for both the self and the world around.

2) Efforts that try to create positive status changes for the self only, without any concern for their effect on the world around.

The first type of activities create *status change*s that normally bring true *positive changes*. These are the primary sources of happiness that create a strong foundation through activities that benefit both the *self* and the world around. They also constitute the eudaimonic sources of happiness as defined by modern psychology. Generally, the activities in the pursuit of this type of happiness try to uplift not only the status of the person creating it, but also the overall status of the greater world around. These *positive changes* can be produced by many different kinds of activities ranging from the dramatic to the everyday regular humdrum activities. They can be physical and/or mental - nothing spectacular is needed. The most important thing is the attitude to create a *positive* ending in whatever we are doing. The next step is to support this attitude with our efforts - whatever effort can be applied comfortably is adequate most of the times.

The second type of *status change*s make up the secondary sources of happiness, commonly known as the *pleasures*. These are basically the hedonistic sources of happiness as classified by modern psychology. The main focus of this type of happiness is self-gratification without much concern for the greater world around. They are generated from activities that produce effects, which are beneficial for the *self*, but can be anything - *positive, neutral* or *negative* for the world around. The activity of eating an ice-cream, for example, or watching an interesting movie delivers pleasure to us, but may not generate any discernable amount of *positive status change*s for the world around. The hedonistic type of happiness can be further subdivided into two groups; let's call them:

a)   hedonistic type A, and

b)   hedonistic type B

The activities in the pursuit of hedonistic type A happiness produce *status change*s that are *positive* for the *self*, and are also *non-negative* for the world around. That is, they are either *positive* or *neutral* for the world around. For example, the act of eating an ice cream produces *status change*s for the *self* in the form of positive sensation through taste; but it produces practically no *status change*s for the world around. Participating in a group sports activity like playing soccer, for example, can be considered as another example of pursuit of mild hedonistic type A happiness, where the acts produce *positive status change*s for the *self*, and also some possible *positive status change*s for the world around. In similar situations where the hedonistic activity creates *positive status change*s for the greater world around, the act can be in the transition zone, from hedonistic to eudaimonic, depending on the purpose.

The activities in the pursuit of hedonistic type B happiness produce *status change*s, which are *positive* for the *self*, but *negative* for the world around. Here the overall *status change* tend to be *negative*. Sexual activities, for example, have the potential of producing tremendous amounts of hedonistic happiness; but depending on the circumstances, they can be either type A or type B. Inappropriate or non-consensual sexual behavior can provide hedonistic type B happiness for the self, while creating significant *negative status change*s for the victims. Business activities of corporations selling products which are harmful for the world while making monetary profits can also be considered as examples of hedonistic type B activities, because here some people benefit at the expense of greater world around. Thus, the activities of selling fossil fuels by the oil and gas industry without any effort to control the resulting global warming may be considered an example of hedonistic type B behavior.

Thus, we can see the clear difference between the eudaimonic and the hedonistic types of happiness - specially between the eudaimonic and the hedonistic type B in terms of the *positive change*s produced by them. If we analyze the destructive activities that are posing the most serious threats to our future survival, we can see that most of them have been created by our activities in the pursuit of hedonistic type B happiness.

But that doesn't mean we have to skip all the hedonistic pleasures - the pleasures of our favorite food or the beautiful music, etc. make the life so rewarding. But, possibly it will wiser to avoid the hedonistic type B as much as possible for the obvious reasons. At its earlier levels, the evolution shows its nature with more purity. If we analyze the activities of the lower animals at the lower levels of evolution, we can see that even though their activities are basically hedonistic in nature, but they are never of the type B. Thus perhaps, the hedonistic type B activities are the ones which are weakening and distorting the nature of our evolution. A healthy and balanced mix of eudaimonic and hedonistic elements in our happiness seem to encourage to create the right kind of routine of activities that generate *positive changes* and thus promote evolution. In today's world, because of its popularity, we are overloading our menu of happiness with the hedonistic types making this mix very unbalanced. Furthermore, many of them are hedonistic type B. Thus, our pursuit of happiness is creating a defective pattern of human activities that are probably causing the majority of serious problems of today's world. Perhaps, here lies the clue to solving some of our most pressing problems that relate to our evolution and our survival in the far future.

(8) Racism

People normally want *positive* things to happen to themselves and to folks of their inner circles. In addition, normal people also like to see good things happen to their community, to their city, to their country and to the world over all, with different degrees of priorities. This attitude of *normalcy* creates his concept of a *positive change*, which is a positive status change for the self, as well as for the greater world around. This is a true *positive change,* and thus normal people will be able to link with happiness through *positive acts.*

On the other hand, people having racist feelings generally wish well for themselves, their close circles and for the people of the same ethnicity; but probably not for people of different ethnicity or kinds. Thus they may lack the attitude for creating *positive changes* for many components of the humanity that make up the human race, and therefore, their concept of a *positive change* may not be overall *positive* for the human race.

Therefore, it is unlikely that it will be possible to build a solid foundation of happiness for the human species with racist philosophies.

(9) Pleasures from the Senses:

Some rewards are given by Mother Nature for just staying alive, probably because staying alive is the most important first step before we can take part in the process of evolution. They are like basic rewards of life. It seems that the list of these pleasures proliferate as the life form climbs higher in the evolutionary ladder. Most sensory pleasures, with some exceptions, belong to this group. For the humans, these rewards are predominantly hedonistic in nature, and generally create very little *positive changes.*

(10) Stress

Stress is generated inside us, when things or events don't happen the way we want them to happen, because of external factors beyond our control, even when we are trying hard. And the level of stress increases when there is the possibility of a harm to us, and the level of perceived harm is significant.

Speaking in terms of *positive changes*, in times of stress, our ability to produce them in the focused area is severely curtailed, causing misery. An alarm is triggered in our mind, and we are urged to focus our attention to that area to fix the problem. But the element, which is causing this problem, is sometimes beyond our control. So, our mental energy can get locked up in that area, but getting no relief and causing misery. The best way to act in this situation might be to give our best effort to fix the problem in that area, but also to look away, and divert our mental energy from this area to other areas, where we can still create *positive changes* and derive happiness.

Many think, the well known serenity prayer[2,3] can be quite useful in managing stress. It says:

"*God*, grant me the serenity to accept the things I cannot change; the courage to change the things I can; and the wisdom to know the difference."

It recommends a similar plan of action.

---

(11) Desire to win and Ego!

We associate an *winner* with superior capabilities. With these capabilities the person has the potential to promote evolution better than others by creating more than the average amounts *positive changes,* and consequently find more happiness than others. This seems to be the objective of all life forms living inside the *force field of life*. Thus we have an instinctive urge to be a winner.

145

In real life, we know that winning equates to earning more money, more fame, and leads to better things in life. But all these positive things happen because as a winner we create more *positive changes* than others. And, we have instinctively created a reward system following Mother Nature's law that *positive changes* are rewarded with happiness. Our system rewards with money or other assets which can be used to buy some form of happiness.

Ego, on the other hand is a blind faith that makes someone assume that he is always *right,* i.e., he is believing that he is always in sync with the *force field of life.* Because his instinct says that being in sync with the *force field of life* is the ideal state of existence. In other words, it makes him believe that his opinions and decisions are always the correct ones, which create the maximum amounts of *positive changes* linking with the maximum amounts of happiness. But this generally is a false assumption, which can prevent the person to acknowledge his flaws and make corrections. This can equate to generation of *negative changes* and invite misery.

The presence of ego also implies that we sense the influence of the *force field of life,* and intuitively know that being in sync with it is the preferred state.

---

(12) Detached Attachment

The practice of detached attachment is the right way to happiness as advised by wise men. Our theory agrees. The *force field of life* is urging all life forms to stay in sync with it. We accomplish this by performing our different activities in the proper ways that create *positive changes.* But sometimes our many emotions and greed tend to throw us off, and prevent us from taking the right decision that could create *positive changes* best. The human history is full of examples of this. Practice of detached attachment may minimize this problem by encouraging logical decision making, and thus increase the possibility of creation of *positive chnages*.

But, arguably, those same emotions that make us illogical, can sometimes strengthen human bonds, and thus create an affectionate environment encouraging production of *positive changes* in other ways. Indiscriminate practice of detachment can damage those bonds, and can create a different kind of problems by favoring the development of vices of different types. If we study the different types of human cultures in different regions of this planet, we may see both systems at work, and their strengths and weaknesses. Thus, perhaps the wise way is to follow whatever generates the most *positive changes* at the specific situation.

(13) Jealousy

Jealousy is generated through comparison; it generally links with unhappiness.

Sam is doing fine in life; he creates his share of *positive changes* through his unique activities that create happiness for him.

John is Sam's neighbor; he also is doing fine. John also finds happiness by creating *positive changes* in his own ways.

Sam thinks John is doing better than him. The thought makes him unhappy - even though he himself is creating enough *positive changes,* and should be happy! Here Sam believes John is creating more *positive changes* than him, and the difference is negative, which is creating the unhappiness.

Jayanta Ghosh

<u>V</u>

(14) The great serenity prayer[2,3]

written by Karl Paul Reinhold Niebuhr may be one of the wisest advices of life. It says:

"God grant me the serenity to accept the things I cannot change; courage to change the things I can; and the wisdom to know the difference."

There are three different segments in the prayer. The first part says:

'God grant me the courage to change the things I can':

Positive changes are constantly being created by our simple everyday activities, but the more significant and noteworthy producers are the courageous activities when risks are taken. They tend to create the *positive* environment. For example, possibly there are some flaws in the systems of our society which are generating *negative changes* for a while. It will take courage and enthusiasm to make changes so that they will start creating *positive changes*.

The second part says:

'accept the things I cannot change':
that is, always strive to create *positive changes*, except when doing it might bring serious harm me. Because self preservation in a *negative* environment is the most important act before we can do anything else.

The third or the last part of the prayer says:

'wisdom to know the difference':
that is, to have the intelligence to know the balance point beyond which the act of creating *positive changes* can be harmful to my well-being. Thus the entire prayer advices us how to create maximum amount of *positive changes,* and consequently happiness.

(15) We feel happy to bond with family members, and friends.

Often in the world, we have to compete against others in our quest of happiness(including pleasures) because, often, we have to find it from common sources. In these situations the support of other people can strengthen our efforts. We feel that family members and friends normally have less chance of competing against us than strangers. Though in real life there are plenty of exceptions, our feeling is instinctive here, which says that chances are better that we will get support from our family members and our friends than from strangers in our pursuit of happiness. There may also be another factor in play very faintly here which is urging us to survive through the different stages of survival and evolution, and be on its forefront. It's like participating in a competition and trying to be a winner. After our death, our family members represent us most closely.

(16) Materialism

Materialism is a culture in which we tend to derive the majority of our happiness from the secondary sources, i.e., from the elements of pleasure. Generally, this type of happiness is more hedonistic[48,49] than eudaimonic[48,49] in nature, i.e., it is generally designed to please the self and its closest circle of people without much concern for the greater world around. But many materialistic objectives contain hidden eudaimonic elements, which benefit the greater world also. There are many examples of this. The great industrial revolution of the 18th and 19th centuries was started pursuing materialism, but it produced many non-materialistic benefits that were enjoyed by the entire world. It uplifted the human civilization providing discoveries and innovations in all areas of human activity. Furthermore, the basic needs seem to be materialistic in nature. Thus, they are vitally important.

But, what people do well beyond the basic needs often can promote or resist our evolution. This effect of promoting or resisting happen mostly in extremely mildly through minute *positive* or *negative changes* created by our activities, and accumulate over very long period of time setting the trend of our evolution. It generally depends on the nature of our activities - whether the activities are generating overall *positive* or *negative changes*. As discussed before, the activities in search of hedonistic happiness can be classified into two groups according to their effects on the greater world around, the hedonistic type A and hedonistic type B. Activities in the pursuit of hedonistic type A are designed to create *positive status changes* for the self(and the close circle), but they are not concerned about benefiting the greater world around, though they also do not harm or create *negative changes* for the greater world. Thus, they may or may not be true *positive changes,* which require *positive* status change for the self and also for the greater world. Activities in the pursuit of hedonistic type B, on the other hand, are designed to benefit the self at the cost of the greater world. Most of the destructive activities are typically generated by hedonistic type B activities. And, materialism uses both, hedonistic type A and type B.

Since materialism has a tendency to seek predominantly hedonistic type of happiness, it has the possibility of creating *negative changes* through the type B activities. Thus, materialism has a direct link with destructive activities, and unless special precautions are taken, often the activities generated through its culture can create overall *negative changes* linking with misery of some type in the future.

A healthy and balanced mix of eudaimonic and hedonistic elements in our happiness seem to encourage to create the right kind of routine of activities that generate *positive changes* and thus promote evolution. In today's world, because of its popularity, we may be overloading our menu of happiness with the hedonistic types, making our mix very unbalanced. Furthermore, many of them are hedonistic type B. Thus, our pursuit of happiness is creating a defective pattern of human activities that may be causing many serious problems of today's world.

Another influence of materialism is that people tend to believe that deeper happiness is found from bigger *toys!* The pleasures from material possessions are mostly hedonistic in nature, and consequently, many of them do not produce much *positive changes*. Also, as we use them more, the sensitivity of the mind to respond to them gradually decreases, and we tend to need bigger and bigger *toys* to derive the same amount of pleasure as before. They can deliver a more intense pleasure temporarily, but soon the level of pleasure comes down to the previous level. So, a larger material possession may not be able to deliver a deeper sustainable happiness, because a larger *positive change* is not there!

(17) Greed

The dictionary defines Greed as:

"a selfish and excessive desire for more of something (as money) than is needed."[12]

Greed tends to alter our sense of priorities.
A normal[1] person, for example, may rank these priorities, on a scale of 10 (10 being most important) in the following way:

Self interests: 7
immediate family's interests: 7
relatives' interests: 4
friends' interests: 4
community's interests: 3
country's interests: 2
world's interests: 1

Through the actions satisfying the perception of priorities, a normal person creates *positive changes* in his world, thus promoting the process of evolution. In return, he receives the rewards of happiness. Greed can alter his priorities, for example to:

Self interests: 9
immediate family's interests: 3
relatives' interests: 0
friends interests: 0
community's interests: 0
country's interests: 0
the world's interests: 0

So, the person's actions can go against the interest of the most of the greater world. What the person may perceive as a positive *change*, may actually be a negative *change* for the rest of the world! This can make the person cause *negative changes* in the greater world around, which in turn can resist the process of evolution, and invite misery to the greater world!

But greed can also be an important element that can make people to apply an extra effort to develop newer capabilities and create *positive changes,* and thus promote evolution and find happiness. Thus, it seems that greed can generate both *positive* and *negative* changes depending on the situation, and, it is up to the people to choose wisely using their attitude and their intelligence. Many of our destructive acts as well as innovations may have been born this way! Thus, a sense of balance seems to be important, which is achieved by knowing when the activities start to generate *negative changes.* Thus, *greed* can be used more efficiently with a mind having a strong sense of *positive change.* But this sense may be instinctive. For the lower animals, it appears that most activities are instinctive; for us, the humans, our advanced intelligence is probably controlling the lion's share of our activities, the sense of positivity, negativity and the boundary line are probably still largely instinctive.

(18) We often get frustrated in trying to find happiness!

Sometimes we are very restless in chasing happiness but not really finding it. One example is in vacation times, when we run from place to place in trying to find the maximum happiness. But often we come back with an unfulfilled, or partially fulfilled feeling! Our subconscious mind says that we have tapped only a small fraction of the happiness available to us, and much still remain untapped!

There is a natural urge in us to get and stay in sync with our *force field of life* through the right activities, and get the maximum happiness possible! This urge has been programmed inside us to promote the process of evolution by creating *positive chnages* as well as we can, and get the most reward. This influence of a force field on its subjects is nicely displayed by the magnetic force field on magnetic compass. It always tries to align itself with the magnetic force field by orienting in the north-south orientation. If we forcibly displace the compass from this north-south orientation, it gets in conflict with the magnetic force field, and turbulence starts through oscillations and vibrations till it gets back to its peaceful, 'happy' state in the north-south orientation. The *force field of life* has a similar effect on us. The unfulfilled feeling will probably be there - no matter what we do, because chances are high that we are never in perfect sync with our *force field of life*! But once we understand this mechanism, and do our activities with a positive attitude (achieved by maintaining a habit of creating *positive changes*), the unfulfilled feeling may disappear, and we may find happiness in many ordinary things.

By the way, the active mind may tend to lean on the unhappy side naturally! This may be because our mind may have an automatic urge to change things towards positive, and thus it may have a list of things to be improved. So, our mind may spend more time on them, than on things that are already *positive*. We worry more about things to be done, rather than feel good because our past accomplishments! The great prayer[2,3] can be very useful here, which says: "God grant me the serenity to accept the things I cannot change; courage to change the things I can and the wisdom to know the difference".

(19) Beliefs and Intelligence:

Beliefs are generally formed from guidance passed on through generations which have proven to be beneficial. *Good* beliefs seem to help people live peaceful lives with good habits, without meaningless feuds. They seem to encourage creation of activities that produce *positive changes*. But they are like empirical data points, which may not be able to cover every situation of life. Sometimes, we may face an unusual situation, which may not be covered by this empirical formula, and it may become difficult to create *positive changes*. Here, intelligence can come into play and find the right acts logically.

(20) Character traits that are helpful for finding happiness.

Happiness in its many different forms is the result of being in sync with the cosmic *force field of life* shrouding our planet. The activities that help us get in sync with the *force field of life* promote the well being and prosperity of life. Thus, the appropriate activities will promote our well being by creating *positive changes*. Most of the activities are created while we are in the pursuit of some type of happiness. The hedonistic type of happiness may produce little or no appreciable amount of *positive changes,* while the eudaimonic type can produce huge amounts of *positive changes,* but the person pursuing it needs to be broad-minded, because here the person will be looking for a positive status change not only for the self but also for the greater world around. Therefore, a broad-minded intelligence that can benefit the self while at the same time also care for the greater world seems to be character trait most useful for finding happiness. The eagerness to pursue the truth is probably another important character trait that may help find happiness. Because this feature help us to become conscious of the presence of the *force field of life* shrouding our planet, try to understand the nature of its influence on us, and then make efforts to try to stay in sync with it with *positive acts.*

(21) Talents, we love and respect

We all know the traditional ways of defining talent. Let's try a different approach. The Sun is radiating immense energy on to our planet, which is creating a tremendous force field, the *force field of life*. It is shrouding our planet, and is casting a strong influence on all life here. We are energized by this force field, and convert part of it into physical and mental energies expressed through our physical and mental activities manifested in many different forms, in ideas, and in actions. Talented people may have a high energy transfer efficiency, which may enable them produce better, innovative ideas to create many more *positive changes* than the average people, and promote evolution more vigorously. And we love, and respect them. Less talented people may have lower efficiency. As a result, they may consume a lot of energy, but then may not transfer well, and create fewer *positive changes*.

(22) Some of the popular political systems

a) Capitalism[8,9]

Capitalism is defined as an economic and political system in which a country's trade and industry are controlled by private owners for profit, rather than by a central government. The ideology sounds great, because it can motivate people to apply their best efforts to find a *profit;* and, application of a vigorous effort is the key to the creation of *positive changes* that promote evolution and deliver us happiness. But the problem can arise from how people define a *profit*.

Profit is generally defined as a *financial gain*, which is materialistic in nature; and beyond the basic needs, a *financial gain* is commonly used to buy items of pleasure, which are generally hedonistic in nature. Thus a *profit* is generally used to spread hedonistic happiness in the world, which most often creates low amounts of *positive changes*. Furthermore, many of them(hedonistic type B as explained before) create *negative changes* culminating in destructive activities. We see many examples of this happening in today's world.

To rectify this situation, the concept of *profit* needs to be changed. A *profit* should represent not just a *financial* gain, but also include many other gains of many other types of elements, which are valuable in human life. But to implement this, a serious cultural change may be needed.

Analyzing the technical features, we see that private ownership is a key feature of Capitalism, in which there is unlimited freedom to find opportunities for personal gains. So, in this system, theoretically, there is tremendous incentive for everyone to create *positive changes* and be rewarded with happiness. Thus this system is similar to the Nature's system of evolution, i.e. a system of giving incentives and producing better results!

But Capitalism has a couple of serious flaws. The first one is that it requires some degree of honesty of recognizing the talents of the people, which, often, may not be followed by the system, and the big fish devours the smaller one. Capitalism thrives on innovative ideas that have the capabilities of creating *positive changes*. It requires that a better idea always has to be given recognition and support. Say, John has an innovative idea. He uses the idea to start a business, and becomes very successful. The company grows and becomes powerful, developing influence over many in the political circles. Then comes Sam with a better idea in the same field of products, and becomes a competitor. Here, for the system to flourish, it is important that Sam should be given recognition and a fair competitive environment. But often this doesn't happen in real life in Capitalism. Most often,

John would try to restrict Sam's growth by using his political power and other unfair ways, and thus resist the process! As a result the production of *positive changes* through a mature capitalist system may be less than expected.

The second flaw is that Capitalism has a tendency to revert to Plutocracy[5], where the government is heavily influenced by a small minority of super wealthy people. In this situation, a small segment of the people of the country, who are extremely wealthy, gain the power to influence the policy makers of the country to make changes in the laws, thus benefiting themselves choking the innovative spirit of the rest of the country. When this happens, the system loses its effectiveness and the capability to create *positive changes*.

The effectiveness of an incentive system depends upon the amount of participation, and the amount of incentive. The participation is extremely important because the amount of *positive changes* generated will depend directly upon the participation. We can formulate this as:

$$E = P.I$$

Were P is the participation index, i.e., the percentage of people able to participate in the system, and I is the incentive index. In the nature's system of evolution, P is wide open to all, and I is also maximum, because of "new experience". In socialist system, for example, I is extremely low, while in an ideal capitalist system it is high. But, in the corrupted capitalist system, as mentioned above, P is low, because a lot of people are kept out of the system by people who have political power. These people successfully entered the room of fortune early, and then shut the door behind them. The value of P also goes low when Capitalism reverts to Plutocracy.

b) Socialism[6,7]

Capitalism and Socialism are located at the opposite ends of the political spectrum. In a socialist system, the state redistributes the wealth of the society in a more equitable way, according to the judgment of the legislator. So, the amount of material incentive available to individuals for creating *positive changes* is almost non-existent. So, this political system promotes evolution only moderately, because the amount of incentive offered to the people who are more talented than the average is limited. The system may be more appropriate in an emergency situation, when there is a disaster, and we just need to survive, or in overcrowded places, where there is not enough food, and necessary materials for everyone. So this system may be more suitable to the countries which are overcrowded and stagnant, and people may just have to survive first with the bare necessities. Here the production of *positive changes* is normally moderate, and so is the availability of happiness.

(23) Praying or worshiping

The master *force field of life* is continuously exerting influence on us, which is urging us to align with it to carry on the super project of positive evolution of life with maximum efficiency. This has created an natural urge inside all of us. This is similar to Earth's magnetic force field exerting it's force on the magnetic compass to align in the north-south orientation. With feel this urge, but vaguely, most of the times.

To fully understand and follow it, we need to cultivate our mind and brain. This requires some work, which may be tough at times. Also, often, thinking on our own, we may not be able to stick to the right path all the time. If we are given a simple formula to follow, this task becomes much easier! Religion may be offering that help, when we may not have to use our brain to choose the right path all the time, and stay with it! In all religious groups, people feel a sense of relief or satisfaction after praying, or worshiping.

But the drawback of this act may lie in the fact that many may feel contented in ritualistic praying and worshiping without really understanding the true meanings of the messages, which may have very useful guidance for creating *positive changes* through our activities. Thus, it may be important to understand the true meaning of the messages preached by religion.

(24) Morality

Recent researches on children give us the hint that some sense of morality may be inborn in human babies somewhat like an instinct. In an experiment, children as young as one-year-olds were shown two dolls, one acted like a good person, while the other doll like a bad person. The children were told to choose one of the two dolls. Surprisingly, 70% children chose the good doll! This may imply that an instinctive process of selection is working in our minds at very early stages of our lives. It makes us lean towards the *good* and away from the *bad*. Analysis easily shows that this instinctive behavior promotes our well being. Normally the activities or the character straits that seem *good* to us also improve our alignment with *force field of life,* and promote the process of evolution by creating *positive changes*. This improves our survival. Following *morality* helps us to grow positively enjoying our lives, and promoting Nature's process of evolution!

In a privacy-loving society, a solid sense of morality seems very important. Because, the love for privacy can cause people to deviate from the "normalcy" gradually, and grow eccentric character traits which may not be able to create *positive changes* that are required for the our evolution and also our happiness in life.

(25) Pleasure of negative gossips

Happiness is found from basically two active sources - either from the pleasures derived from materialistic elements, or by the creation of *positive changes* in our world. Most of the time, we use a combination of the two. But there is another way of finding a form of happiness, which is passive and quite popular. This is achieved by comparing one's status with that of others around. Generally, the base of comparison is made from the apparent status of people, who are generally our friends, peers, neighbors, and even relatives. Their status is lowered, often in a make-believe way, by exaggerating their flaws and their problems through gossips, which make the status of the gossiper look better in comparison. This virtual comparative improvement in the status of the gossiper delivers the person a passive sense of happiness. The activity is quite popular in society probably because it does not need much effort. But this happiness is transitory in nature, because most often it is not based on facts, and also the activity doesn't improve the status of the gossiper. But it can discourage people to get active in the pursuit of happiness the right way.

But the activity is not totally without merits. If the gossip is based on facts, it can indirectly generate *positive changes* by circulating a sense of reality in the environment, when people can create positive change of status.

(26) The strategy of non-violence:

Mahatma Gandhi's famous philosophy of non-violence[4,10] helps people minimize the intensity of the opposing force while preserving its own intensity, and focus on the objective by not getting distracted. This helps to create a bigger net effort for the creation of *positive changes*.

In original Sanskrit, the philosophy quoted the word "ahimsa", which has been equated to "non-violence" in English. But the word "ahimsa" has a bigger meaning. It also forbids negative feelings like "jealousy", and acts of "revenge", both of which tend to create *negative changes*. Jealousy can have a canceling effect on positive forces, and taking revenge is the act of responding to a negative act by another negative act.

(27) Sometimes people are doing good things, but still are unhappy!

This typically happens when we are eager to find happiness, but do not know its true mechanism - we are not aware of the fact that happiness does not depend on the occurrence of big material gains or big occasions. It depends upon the creation of *positive changes,* which can be accomplished through simple regular daily activities.

The *force field of life* is casting a strong influence on all life, and is urging us to align with it. We achieve this by promoting its project of evolution by creating *positive changes* through our activities. The return is the happiness of some type. The knowledge of this science can give us a sense of direction for our activities of life, and also the resulting conviction we need.

―――――

(28) Transition between generations

Youth is a great time of Life - the time of plenty. But during this period, just as the abundant energy and enthusiasm of youth can enrich our civilization, and promote the process of evolution, its false sense of invincibility can also magnify the lack of foresight, and its destructiveness! This is the time of life when the work of tuning up of the mind needs to be done for use in later years when the person may need to be more efficient with his/her efforts to create *positive changes.*

So, helping the youth with the proper guidance to develop his/her mind property, is an act of promoting the process of evolution. We are evolving with time, and the wisdom is passed on to the next generation like passing the torch of life. But there has to be a effective bond between generations, so that we can hold hands strongly and communicate well, while enjoying our journeys thru life, passing on the wisdom, and helping us evolve. That's why, one of the most important requirements of a superior culture, would be the presence of a good bond between generations built with care, love and nurture for the creation of *positive changes.*

―――――

(29) Fairness is not an attribute of the kind soul, but a requirement of Nature:

We often think that an act of *fairness* is an optional virtuous act from a kind soul! But in reality it may be an intelligent act of the thinking mind. With the help of *fairness*, we can detect and appreciate the qualities in others, and help them grow to their potential, and produce *positive changes* that benefit all. Thus, fairness links with happiness.

Fairness seems to be a requirement of Nature for creation of the proper environment that will encourage the emergence of true leaders from all segments of population without prejudice or discrimination. This boosts the production of *positive changes* that promote evolution and create an environment of happiness.

V

(30) We tend to get less happy as we get older!

The *force field of life* is continually giving us rewards in the form of happiness of different types for staying in sync with it through our activities. These acts promote evolution by creating *positive changes*. When we are in the prime of our lives, we obviously can perform better, and create larger amounts of *positive changes* in many areas of life than when we are older. In this context, reproduction of species is probably the next most important issue after the act of self preservation through eating of food. Accordingly, a huge reward of pleasure is attached to the activities of reproduction, which are predominantly the activities of the youth.

Most of the easily available and intense rewards of happiness are acquired in the youthful years of our lives. As we get older, many of those rewards start to fade, and make us unhappy. But, there is one solid silver lining in this gloomy backdrop - it is possible that the mind is developed to be more mature and wiser, so that it is more efficient in selecting the activities that will create *positive changes* to find happiness. In fact, it may be possible to develop a mind to reach such a state that it finds much more happiness in older years than in younger years, because the youth is often very wasteful!

Though, *positive changes* can be created by helping people in general, one of the most effective ways of creating them is by helping the needy youth, who probably have the greatest impact on the future of the human race, and thus the amount of *positive change* created should be very high.

(31) Happiness from religion

At the dawn of human civilization, people felt the presence of a supreme force as we still feel today. They didn't understand this force fully well, but experienced its power and influence through occurrences in nature, and also through life experiences. People named this supreme force, *God*. The cosmic *force field of life* shrouding this planet, the creator of all life here, also has very similar attributes. Thus, *God* appears to be the same as the *force field of life*, and *pleasing God* is same as staying in sync with the *force field of life*. Thus, following the advices of religion is basically same as staying in sync with the *force field of life* through our activities, which create *positive changes* and consequently promote evolution.

Thus, religion and spirituality can offer valuable guidance in our pursuit of happiness that help us generate *positive changes* in our world and find happiness. But sometimes this great help can be difficult to obtain because of various reasons including lack of enough conviction, improper interpretation of the messages, questionable preaching etc., when its ability to generate *positive changes* and consequently find happiness can be impaired. The lack of conviction seem to originate from the fact that the messages of religion do not use the support of logic and science. Also, in the name of *pleasing God* we sometimes get involved in ritualistic and superstitious activities which produce very little *positive changes*, and do not invite lasting happiness! Thus, a better option may be to worship any way we like, but always strive to create *positive changes* in our world through our daily activities.

(32) Follow Religion with blind faith or with logic and intelligence!

Activities recommended by religion are supposed to be able to link with happiness because they are capable of creating a great deal of *positive changes*. But, the history shows that time to time the messages of religion fail to encourage the expected right kind of activities because of various reasons. These include misinterpretation, flawed preaching, and other elements causing deviation from the right path and the resulting lack of generation of *positive changes*.

This may be prevented if people use logic and intelligence along with their devotion. Then they may be alerted whenever a preaching creates a *negative change*. Thus, it may be wiser and safer to practice a religion with our mind and brain, than with our mind and blind faith! This way we may be able to generate *positive changes*, while avoiding the *negative* ones.

(33) Good Friends, Bad Friends, Enemies!

Good friends are in sync with each other, so that they unite their resources to apply a larger effort to create *positive changes* in the world around to increase the happiness to them and their friends.

Bad friends may be in sync with each other, but their joint effort is not focused to create *positive changes* in the world around. It may help them find more elements of pleasures, the secondary source of happiness. But most often this happiness is shallow and temporary. And, the lack of *positive changes* in their efforts make them vulnerable for misery in the long run. Thus the company of bad friends is generally not helpful for finding happiness.

Enemies try to reduce our capabilities to create *positive changes*, because they try to restrict our efforts causing probability of misery to both sides depending on relative strengths.

(34) Grief from the death of a friend or a relative

We expect supports from our relatives and friends in our efforts. Thus, when one of them passes away, we instinctively feel the loss.

(35) Loyalty

Being loyal to someone is like following somebody blindly. The loyal person follows and supports the leader's every move as much as possible. So, this way the follower trusts the leader's decision making in his/her activities for the creation of *positive changes* for finding happiness. Thus the loyal person's happiness or misery is significantly influenced by the quality of the person followed.

---

(36) Love of Privacy

Privacy lets us pursue any subject with less interruption, and more focus, in our quest for happiness. It can enable us to concentrate our efforts to create a *positive change* without direct contact with other people, e.g. creating an idea or a theory. So, this way privacy can link to happiness.

Privacy can also enable us to enjoy the elements of pleasure more freely without inhibitions, or interruptions; so the degree of happiness out of them may be more intense. Moreover, the range of sources of pleasure can be extended to include unusual items. But, in these situations, the sources of pleasure normally are hedonistic in nature, which have limited capabilities for producing *positive changes*. Furthermore, as mentioned before, the hedonistic type B elements can give rise to destructive acts, which can link with misery in the big picture.

Privacy can also have a significant flaw. It can gradually change the concept of normalcy, which in turn, can distort the concept of the *positive change*, and deviate from creating happiness for the world around. This is why, it may be extremely crucial for privacy loving people to maintain a strong sense of normalcy, to be able to create *positive changes*, while avoiding the negative ones. A solid sense of morality can help to maintain a good sense of normalcy.

---

(37) Death and the feeling of loss

A few years ago a very dear friend of mine passed away; he was also my brother-in-law. We had many great times together. I was severely grief stricken. It was specially painful, because he seemed to have a premonition that he was not going to make it, and wanted to see me, but I couldn't be there at the time of his death. This sad feeling had been lingering in my mind, when one night I had a dream:

I saw him telling me, "Don't be sad. I'm really not gone - I am still all around you. The stuff that I was made of, are all there around you. So, please don't be sad any more". On waking up, I felt an inexplicable relief, and strangely, never felt that grief again!

On this planet we all are interrelated and bonded to each other. We receive our elements of happiness through many sources, some of which come through the relationships with many other people, mostly friends and relatives. It is like having many windows of happiness, some of which are common with other people. So when one of them dies, a common window of happiness closes, and we feel the sense of loss as grief.

It seems logical that this sense of loss can be minimized by opening new windows through mental/physical activities. Therefore, if we realize the truth about death, and then we try to create new windows of happiness to make up for the lost ones, we may be in good shape. There may be many possibilities of accomplishing this. The best ways would be the ones which have the highest possibilities of creating the most *positive changes*. One of them may be in helping people - specially in helping the youth. The young people have the most vigor and longevity to create *positive changes* with their activities. And, there are many programs dealing with young people needing help.

We are all independent, and yet related and bonded to each other by being part of the same energy source. We live our time, called life, in the timeframe of the process of evolution; and when we are too worn out to be able to play our role well, a fresh player takes our place. But the team of life forms keeps on playing the same game of life and evolution. Its like a big machine keeps on running. Sometimes, some of its parts may wear out, and get replaced by new ones. I think it would be kind of foolish if we grieve too much for a part when the main body is still going strong, and working for a purpose!

As we get old, aches and pains of the aging body parts tend to keep our minds busy for a large part of our time, and take away some or a lot of our happiness. If we can take our mind away from the pains, and be able to focus on something pleasurable, we may be able to find more happiness. But, it may be easier said than done. We may need a stronger mind, and I think regular meditation can be very helpful here.

(38) We naturally love to be with others in harmony:

Mother Nature wants us to carry on her project of evolution. We all possess an energy to promote it. But when we unite harmoniously, our power to create *positive change*, and thus to promote evolution increases, and as a result we get rewarded with deeper happiness.

(39) Why do we love music

Summer is followed by winter, and then summer again. Night comes after day, and then night again. Some birds migrate from south to north in the Spring, and back to south in the Fall in very precise times of the year, and repeats this cycle every year. Other migratory animals repeats similar cycles precisely. Non-migratory animals also change their lifestyles in precise cycles in the year, and repeat the cycle every year.

Mother Nature is cyclical or rhythmic in nature. Animals had to synchronize their living styles with the rhythm of forces of Mother Nature from the very early stages of evolution in order to survive. If they ignore these cycles, they probably would perish because of ignoring the rhythm of Nature. As animals passed through the different phases of the evolution, their sense of rhythm progressively got stronger and more complex, and finally might have helped develop the sense of music in a human.

A child probably gets introduced to this rhythm of Nature from his/her mother's heartbeat inside her womb, starting at the early stage of conception. The ability to feel the rhythm may be getting imprinted in our genes, which started many evolutionary steps ago, and got only stronger with every phase of evolution and has become more intense and precise.

(40) The family that invites happiness

The structure of the family can be of a few different kinds. Let's consider that there are three generations of people in the family – children, their parents, and their grandparents.

In the first type, they all live independently and separately. The parents live in their home with their children; the grandparents live on their own in a separate home. The children move out as soon as they are adults, and support themselves. The generations are detached and independent. In this situation, the people of different generations get their happiness from the *positive changes* created basically by their own activities only. They normally do not unify their resources to produce a larger *positive change,* but they also do not waste their resources by infighting. As a result, the happiness in this family may be clearly defined but limited. It is dependent on their own activities.

In the second type, a large family is made up of three generations living together, either under the same roof, or some other living arrangements close to each other. But they don't live harmoniously, and feud with each other constantly, and consequently use up a considerable part of their resources in quarrels. As a result, they use only a small part of their available energy in creating *positive changes*. Here, probabilities are high that their happiness index is smaller than that of the first type.

In the third type, the large family of the above example live together harmoniously. Each member of the family contributes in taking care of household chores in a disciplined way, and has a unique role in the activities of the family. They care for each other, and a strong bond is present in the family. The grandparents are wanted and respected. In turn, they enrich the family with their affection and experience creating an environment, which is conducive for *positive change*s to happen. When it is time to go, the older generation pass on their torch of wisdom and life experiences to the younger generation with the minimum transfer loss. This seems to be the ideal structure of a family that can promote evolution most efficiently. As a result, they seem to have the potential to generate the highest amount of *positive changes*, and find the most happiness.

(41) The direction of life's natural flow

If we look at our history the past few hundred years, we may be able to see the *positive changes*, *negative changes*, and the overall trend of our civilization.

Some of the most important *positive changes* are:

a) We, the human race, have improved our capabilities tremendously to survive on this planet by developing our Science and Technology by leaps and bounds.

b) We have advanced our knowledge of the universe, our real neighborhood, and have started to get familiarized with it.

The most serious issue that is creating *negative changes* is that our destructive activities are increasing rapidly and have accumulated to an alarming level. Some of the most damaging are:

a) Overpopulation

b) Extreme Pollution

c) Global Warming

The overpopulation problem may be largely due to the lack of good political leadership. The problems in the other two areas can be attributed to selection of the wrong type of happiness as the reward for our activities. As we have discussed before, *happiness* can be classified into three types on the basis of the *positive changes* created by the activities which create the *happiness*:

a) Eudaimonic

b) Hedonistic Type A

c) Hedonistic Type B

The Eudaimonic happiness create *positive changes* for the person creating it(self), as well as for the greater world around. Thus, it is truly the best type for building a strong foundation of happiness. The Hedonistic Type A happiness is designed to create *positive changes* for the self only. It may or may not generate *positive changes* for the greater also, but it won't generate *negative changes* for the greater world. The Hedonistic Type B happiness, on the other hand, generates *positive changes* for the self, but *negative changes* for the world around. Thus, this may be the *wrong* type of happiness, and most of the destructive activities are formed when we are in the pursuit of Hedonistic Type B happiness. And unfortunately, this seems to be quite popular in today's human cultures.

It may be possible to check the health of our culture by checking to see how closely it follows the ideal path - the path that creates *positive changes,* and thus tries to stay in sync with the *force field of life.* This can be done by checking to see if the people who create the most *positive changes* have the power to influence the society, so that they can lead the people in the right direction!

<hr>

Is there an even bigger purpose for the *force field of life!*

Hope, we all can acknowledge the presence of this supreme *cosmic force field of life* shrouding our planet, and understand its influence on us. Hope, we can understand the mechanism of *happiness,* and realize that the foundation of happiness is most soundly built by creating *positive changes* through the activities of our lives - however extremely minute those *changes* may be! By accomplishing this, we can promote the process of evolution, and in return, enjoy the rewards called *happiness* in its many different forms, without creating unnecessary destructive acts. As we evolve, we can see that there exists an even deeper purpose for life and the presence of the pleasant feeling called *happiness* that can link with the survival of our species as a living entity in the huge universe! There may be many other purposes as well. For example, let's picture this:

A space known as our Universe contains many energy sources of tremendous magnitude. These energies keep on transferring from one form to other, mostly haphazardly. For example, an explosion happens - the resulting fire and the heat turn mostly into sound, motion and light, and then through an impact, into sound, motion, light, and heat again. These processes keep on repeating randomly. Let's call these *direct energy transfers*. But over millions of years, in this energy soup, a unique product is born. It starts some remarkably different ways of energy transfers and energy management! This product is made of an unique blend of materials, surrounding a fragment of the same cosmic energy in the core! It is the living organism! It starts to convert, and manage the energy in a truly different way. It absorbs a small amount of energy, uses part of it to run its internal organs, and then converts it into other conventional forms - motion, heat, sound, etc. But the most surprising thing is that it can propagate itself, and gradually evolve higher with progressively more capabilities as a living entity of the universe!

Over a time of millions of years, this living being evolves into today's human and develops capabilities to perform a complex plan of the cosmic energy management. He can use the energy, originally from the sun, use part of it to run his organs, nourish his brain, and other parts of the body, and make energy transfers into other forms. In addition, most importantly, he can develop a plan to manage energy somewhere in the universe, or in another planet remotely, e.g. move an object, or cause an explosion in another planet in the solar system, etc.. This is a complex and non-linear way of managing the cosmic energy.

If we look at this change in the ways of energy transfers from the simple, linear earlier processes to complex non-linear processes, we can see a clear trend, developing over millions of years. It is the trend of more and more advanced ways of management, and utilization of the tremendously abundant cosmic energy around us! And it has speeded up exponentially in the last 200 years of evolution.

Perhaps, some day the techniques can be developed to such an advanced state that the humans will achieve something of truly significant importance by making it possible to manage, and utilize this energy to make inter-galactic trips, or move into another planet, and become a living entity of the universe when our earth is no longer livable. But the question is whether the humans will have enough time on this earth to develop their technology to that advanced state, or they will destroy this mother ship with all her occupants by their careless actions, before that time! It is logically possible that similar situations have happened in some other planets in the huge galaxy in the past! It is possible that some planets may have passed this test of survival, and extended their presence in the galaxy, while some others perished and have become dead planets!

We may be able to save our mother planet until that time if we live properly, by focusing our energy to *positive* activities, avoiding destructive acts and wasteful in-fights. And, the simple rules explained in this book may be able to help us by providing the guidelines to pursue happiness properly. But, we might have arrived at a critical point in our journey through evolution, where, according to science, the accumulations of destructive acts in some areas may be approaching the points of no return! And, time is passing.

References

1 normal people: dictionary.ref.com/browse/normal

2 Justin Kaplan, ed., *735 (17ʰ ed. 2002) (attributing the prayer to Niebuhr in 1943).*

3 *The Essential Reinhold Niebuhr: Selected Essays and Addresses*, Reinhold Niebuhr, edited by Robert McAfee Brown, page 251, Yale University Press; New Ed edition (September 10, 1987)

4 Nicholas F. Gier (2004). *The Virtue of Nonviolence: From Gautama to Gandhi.* SUNY Press. p. 222.

5 Plutocrats: The Rise of the New Global Super-Rich and the fall of Everyone Else, Chrystia Freeland

6 The ABC of Communism, Nicoli Bukharin, 1920, Section 20

7 Socialism, Britannica ACADEMIC EDITION

8 Capitalism, Oxford Dictionaries

9 Capitalism, Encyclopedia Britannica

10 Gandhi's Philosophy of Ahimsa and its application to current conflicts. Newsblaze.com (2007-10-14). Retrieved on 2011-06-15.

11 CNN news article by Susan Chun, dated Fri February 14, 2014 (http://www.cnn.com/2014/02/12/us/baby-lab-morals-ac360/)

12 The definition in Merriam-Webster dictionary

13 The Origin of Species by Charles Darwin and Julian Huxley

14 Are we born with a moral core? The Baby Lab says 'yes' by Susan Chun, CNN, Updated 9:40 PM ET, Fri February 14, 2014

15 Nondualism: A Brief History of a Timeless Concept by Michael Taft

16 Gavin Flood (1998), An Introduction to Hinduism, Cambridge University Press, ISBN 978-0521438780, page 92-93

17 Klaus Klostermaier, Moksha and Critical Theory, Philosophy East and West, Vol. 35, No. 1 (Jan., 1985), pages 61-71

18 Andrew Fort and Patricia Mumme (1996), Living Liberation in Hindu Thought, ISBN 978-0-7914-2706-4 ^

19 Norman E. Thomas (April 1988), Liberation for Life: A Hindu Liberation Philosophy, Missiology, Volume 16, Number 2, pp 149-160 ^

20 Gerhard Oberhammer (1994), La Délivrance dès cette vie: Jivanmukti, Collège de France, Publications de l'Institut de Civilisation Indienne. Série in-8°, Fasc. 61, Édition-Diffusion de Boccard (Paris), ISBN 978-2868030610, pages 1-9

21 Comans, Michael (2000), The Method of Early Advaita Vedanta: p183

22 HM Vroom (1989), Religions and the Truth: Philosophical Reflections and Perspectives, Eerdmans Publishing, ISBN 978-0802805027, pages 122-123

23 Frederic F Fost (1998), Playful Illusion: The Making of Worlds in Advaita Vedanta, Philosophy East and West, Vol. 48, No. 3, pages 388, 397 and note 11

24 M. V. Nadkarni (2016). The Bhagavad-Gita for the Modern Reader: History, interpretations and philosophy

25 Hargreaves, Adam D.; Swain, Martin T.; Hegarty, Matthew J.; Logan, Darren W.; Mulley, John F. (1 August 2014). "Restriction and Recruitment—Gene Duplication and the Origin and Evolution of Snake Venom Toxins". Genome Biology and Evolution. 6 (8): 2088–2095. doi:10.1093/gbe/evu166. ISSN 1759-6653. PMC 4231632. PMID 25079342.

26 Evolution Resources". Washington, DC: National Academies of Sciences, Engineering, and Medicine. 2016. Archived from the original on 2016-06-03.

27 Patrick Olivelle (2014), The Early Upanishads, Oxford University Press, ISBN 978-0195124354

28 King, Richard (1995), Early Advaita Vedanta and Buddhism: the Mahayana context of the Gaudapadiya-karika, Gaudapada, State University of New York Press, ISBN 978-0-7914-2513-8

29 Lawsuits Lay Bare Sackler Family's Role in Opioid Crisis
The New York Times, April 1, 2019

30 Former Sales Exec Says Opioid Maker Insys Bribed Doctors to Prescribe Drugs
NBC News, March 1, 2019

31 Misinformation from Drug Companies Fueled Opioid Problem
The Newnan Times-Herald (Newnan, Ga.), February 26, 2019

32 Senate Democrats Question Financial Ties Between HHS Advisers and Opioid Manufacturers
Modern Healthcare, December 19, 2018

33 Opioid Prescription Doses Outpace Patient Usage
HospiMedica.com, November 28, 2018

34 Patients Receive More Opioids than Necessary After Surgery, Study Shows
Everyday Health, November 12, 2018

35 Surgical Patients Receive Four Times the Opioids They Use, Study Shows
Modern Healthcare, November 8, 2018

36 NIH; National Institute of Health; Drug overdose deaths, 2017

37 Karen Pechelis (2014), The Embodiment of Bhakti, Oxford University Press.

38 Robert A. McDermott (1975), Indian Spirituality in the West: A Bibliographical Mapping, Philosophy East and West, University of Hawai'i Press, Vol. 25, No. 2 (Apr 1975), pp. 228-230

39 Mihaly Csikszentmihályi (1990). Flow: The Psychology of Optimal Experience. Harper & Row. ISBN 978-0-06-016253-5.

40 Swami Vivekananda, Raja Yoga, ISBN 978-1500746940

41 Jason Birch (2013), Rājayoga: The Reincarnations of the King of All Yogas, International Journal of Hindu Studies, Volume 17, Issue 3, pages 401–444

42 Timothy Burgin: Jnana Yoga: The Yoga of Wisdom; Yoga Basics.

43 "Upanishad". Random House Webster's Unabridged Dictionary.

44 Snow, Michael J.,. Mindful philosophy. Milton Keynes. ISBN 9781546292388

45 Aditya Thakur (1 November 2014). "Just A Handful Of Hindus Know Adi Shankaracharya Revived Their Religion". Topyaps. Retrieved 16 May 2014

46 Shankara | Indian philosopher". Encyclopedia Britannica.

47 Rosenbloom, Stephanie (August 7, 2010). "But Will It Make You Happy?". The New York Times. Retrieved August 16, 2010.

48 Brickman; Campbell (1971). Hedonic relativism and planning the good society. New York: Academic Press. pp. 287–302. in M. H. Apley, ed., Adaptation Level Theory: A Symposium, New York: Academic Press

49 Hedonia, eudaimonia, and well-being: an introduction. Edward L. Deci &; Richard M. Ryan. Nov 18, 2006

50 Happy: 2011 feature documentary film written, directed and co-produced by Roco Belic.

V

Printed in the United States
by Baker & Taylor Publisher Services